HR
Questions
with
401 Answers
&
Tips

Gyan Shankar

Content

Chapter 1

Situational Interview Questions

Q. Tell me about a time you had to work alongside a difficult co-worker.

Tips: The hiring manager wants to see how you work with others by asking this question. They also want to know you can resolve conflict on your own, when possible.

Model answer: In my role as a marketing assistant, I worked with a copywriter who was frequently absent from work. This made completing assignments on time difficult. Instead of dwelling on my frustration, I had a conversation with her. I found out she was caring for her mother, who was sick. We worked together to adjust our workflow and shift deadlines to ensure she had plenty of notice for upcoming assignments, making it easier for her to work ahead and prioritize. Once we were on the same page, we were able to communicate better, and we even started meeting our deadlines an average of two days early! Our manager was thrilled.

Q.   Describe a time when you failed. How did you overcome this?

Tips: This can feel like a jarring question; after all, you're being asked to expose a weakness. However, use this as an opportunity to highlight the skills and experience you used to bounce back from this failure. Don't dwell on the failure part of the question too much; instead, focus on the positive outcome.

Model answer: As a content manager, I was responsible for overseeing the team's editorial calendar, keeping tabs on deadlines, and posting new articles to the website. One time I accidentally made a mistake and let a sponsored post written for one of our largest clients slip through the cracks, and I missed the deadline to get it on our website.

I realized my mistake the next morning, and I immediately took the steps I needed to remedy it. I posted the story as quickly as possible, and I took ownership and apologized directly to the client. After that, I suggested we refine our workflow, so this wouldn't happen again. I pinpointed weaknesses in the process and found ways to fix them. With the improvements we made, we hit every deadline 100 per cent of the time after that!

Q.   You're assigned a task you don't know how to complete. What do you do?

Tips: With this question, an interviewer wants to gauge your ability to work independently, problem-solve, and take initiative.

Model answer: When I started my job as a data analyst at AB Co-op, I was the first person who ever held this position. I didn't have many training documents, and I didn't have concrete direction from management.

Instead of waiting for someone to tell me what to do, I immediately began sitting in on various team meetings so I could get a better understanding of the company's product, sales, and marketing strategy. I asked team members what type of data they needed, and I helped them understand how they could benefit from using data.

With these insights, I took this as an opportunity to apply my 10 years of experience with other companies and develop a plan of action. It took a few months to settle in, but with the insights I provided the team, we increased our sales by 90 per cent the first quarter I was there.

Q. Where do you see yourself in 5 years?

Tips: Tell them that you wish to learn about and master a specific technology. You should be able to persuade them that you intend to stay with the organization for a longer time. "I want to be more skilled, more confident, and maintain a prominent position in your firm," you might remark. For seasoned professionals, you can begin by saying, "Within the next five years, I want to be recognized as an authority in this subject." The recruiter is solely interested in learning how long you expect to stay with the company and how happy you are with the current role for which you will be employed.

Q. What is your salary expectation?

Tips: This is a difficult one. You may or may not opt to quote the actual amount, but you must inform them of the percentage raise you are considering. Don't ask for a certain salary; instead, demonstrate your devotion to the position.

Q. What is the starting salary for freshers in Deloitte?
Ans. The starting salary for freshers at Deloitte averages around 4.5 lakhs per annum.

Q. Why should we hire you Deloitte?
Tips: The interviewer is trying to figure out whether you'd be a good fit for their company. As a result, you'll have to convince them.

Ans. I am a quick learner who can swiftly assimilate something new to me," is how you can frame it. Here you can talk about your abilities, skills, and past experiences, as well as how you can add something new to the role.

Q. What are your strengths and weaknesses?
Tips: Here, be honest about your strengths and weaknesses. You may have several strengths but concentrate on the ones that will aid you in this position. Mention your flaw in the same way. Be

sure to express how you plan to overcome your weakness as soon as you acknowledge it.

The following are some examples of strengths that can be addressed in an interview: -

Versatile and goal-oriented.

The ability to communicate.

Pressure-handling ability

Ability to lead.

Some of the flaws that people mention in an interview are listed below.

Excessive attention to detail.

Anxiety about speaking in front of a group.

Self-critical.

Q. How do you handle stress or tight deadlines?

Tips: Employers are looking for instances of how stressful conditions motivate you or how you may minimize stressful situations with proper planning and good communication skills. Give an example of how you dealt with a challenging scenario at a previous job to demonstrate your ability to perform under pressure

Chapter 2

Job Fitness Questions

Q. What interests you about our company?

Sample Ans.: I have done research and studied a lot about your company. It has an excellent image, and its message is persuasive. Internally, it's a sound operation, with ambitious goals and realistic plans for achieving them. I see great potential for growth here, and I want to be part of it I have many ideas that I know could be implemented here better than anywhere else.

Q. What single thing about our product or service interests you most?

Sample Ans.: To structure your reply few illustrative sentences are given here:
1. I understand your.......... systems have the least maintenance downtime of any on the market.
2. For a sales executive, that's an important advantage. You're offering the customers more value and efficiency for their investment.
3. You just introduced an innovative motor vehicle insurance package, and you're the only company in the industry that offers so much premium flexibility. I'd like to be able to work with a progressive organization whose products offer its customers the leading edge in insurance protection.

Q. Why did you apply to our company?

Sample Ans.: I applied to your company because your team is making life easier and more enjoyable for people. The scale of your work is tremendous, and I feel like my work here can have a real positive impact. I also love the company culture and how there's a focus on teamwork and collaboration.

Q. What special traits do you have that make

Are you well-suited to this job?

Sample Ans.: I'm punctual, and organized, get along well with people, and am supremely diligent. There is so much information, all around us, that can help us do our jobs so much better if we simply bother to read it and observe the works. I have been able to sell through an idea simply by referring to some fact or acquired knowledge.

Q. What is your aim in life?

Sample Ans.: Presently, my goal is to become an integral part of a reputed organization where I can enrich my real-world skills and take on new challenges. I want to apply my knowledge and skills to contribute to an organization's growth and success. Most importantly, I want to be happy and satisfied with my job. As for my long-term goals, I wish to build a comfortable life for myself and my family.

Q. What are your short-range and long-range goals?

Sample Ans.: My immediate goal, humble as it may sound, is to start at this position of your agency. My long-range goal is to grow to be known as an authority in this profession. But as that's probably years down the road, right now, I'm keen to start at this or a higher position as you deem fit.

Q. What are your biggest achievements?

Sample Ans.: In March, last year, I had already planned scheduled activities for my targeted job. I was asked by our head office in Singapore to upgrade all of our office computers to a new software package in a week, without disrupting the normal work. We have over 600 computers across four locations. I held meetings with senior managers to persuade them that it was important. I had to coordinate the efforts of my team to ensure that all of the computers were upgraded within those few days. It took a lot of planning and hard work, but I was proud of the fact that we managed the migration and had only a few minor problems – and no complaints from the staff.

Q. How have you set and managed your goals?

Sample Ans.: I had to figure out my strengths and set life goals. I found myself to be logical, articulate, resourceful and enjoy solving problems. These strengths led me to pursue a double major in political science and history. Then, I went to law school. I started as an associate at "XYZ", a law firm; but couldn't take the ninety-hour weeks. So, after a couple of years, I moved over to the corporate side and became an associate at "ABLANCO" Systems. After three years at this post, I decided that I was more suited to a job in business development. "ABLANCO" encouraged me to make the switch, and for the following three years, I helped the company look for acquisitions. I find that business development enables me to use all of my natural talents, and it's my goal to continue to pursue my calling at your firm.

Q. What is the most difficult thing that you've ever accomplished?

Sample Ans.: I changed the corporate culture of the company where I was working. When I first arrived, there was a suffocating work culture. Everyone kept their doors closed all day long. I sent out a memo to the entire staff saying that, immediately we will have an open-door policy. There were two great results of the open-door policy. The first was that I had a chance to find out what people's issues were with the company. The second was that everyone started leaving their doors open, and morale improved 100 per cent.

Q. Your recent achievement that you're proud of?

Sample Ans.: At the call, door to door delivery program that I implemented boosted package sales by 30 per cent.

Q. Can you describe a time when you felt under pressure to perform? What was the outcome?

Sample Ans.: Certainly. I was new to the company. I was ordered to attend a high-power meeting of an associate company. There were some accounting discrepancies that I noticed, and so I practically assaulted the CFO with question after question. I reported the issue to my senior. As a result, we ended up doing more due diligence on that company than we had ever done before. Our company walked away from further investment in that company, and I was rewarded with a huge bonus that year.

Q. Why do you think you are qualified for this job? It's not like you have any previous experience.

Sample Ans.: Well, I have a great deal of life experience. My counselling and coaching on the weekends show my ability to relate to people at all different age levels. I have also become very involved in the PTA, which often requires calming down irate people. I helped my school launch an internship program, spearheaded by both the parents and the alumni. This involved my management skills, people-assessment skills, and genuine persistence. My interest in human resources led me to go for academic and professional qualifications in Human Resources. Are there any other skills that you feel the job requires, I will acquire them while working with you.

Q. What do you view as your risks and disadvantages with the position we are interviewing you for?

Sample Ans.: My role requires immediate at-the-stop decisions on even matters that may have long-term implications. My home office is located halfway across the globe where my boss and other senior management peroneal are sitting. Despite, all communication facilities like teleconferencing, video conferencing, email etc, if there ever happens a communication breakdown with the key decision makers, I have to decide to handle the issue, if it somehow backfires, I even may be fired from the job for that. Still, I like to take on the responsibilities of the job as it involves risk and challenges.

Q. Your resume states that you have management experience. Do you realize that you wouldn't be managing anyone at this company? And how do you feel about that?

Sample Ans.: Let me face it. I have a tenacity to adapt to change. I have indeed managed people in the past. Managing is about organizing meeting deadlines, and having good people skills to motivate groups of people to get things done in a time frame. These skills will serve your company well, even though your management structure is flat, loose, and dynamic. I'll have a lot more time in my day to get my real work done.

Q. Can you see yourself working for several demanding bosses in different teams at this company?

Sample Ans.: Yes, I can see myself happily juggling the demands of several different bosses. It will be my pleasure to work with demanding bosses. I fully expect to put in the time, pay my dues, and learn from the best in the business. Most of my bosses have sincerely appreciated my approach to working under pressure. Can you tell me a little bit more about who I would be working for and the structure of your organization, so I can show you that I'm the best person for this job?

Q. Are you sure that you want to work here? I mean, you seem pretty talented. And take it from me, there are firms out there that are a lot better.

Sample Ans.: A. Well, I'm sorry to hear that you don't exactly love me here. But I've always wanted to work here because your company has a great reputation, wins clients, gets written up in the trades consistently, has a charismatic CEO and manages to do well year after year, according to your company's Annual Report. Still, I'm curious about your experience…what are some of the setbacks that you've encountered in the past two years?

Q. Do you like to work with facts and figures?

Sample Ans.: A. I like and consider facts and figures very important for the company. I'm good with them, but I don't get bogged down in them. I always read the reports, and I'm quick to spot inconsistencies and errors. I don't check every number twice, though, because that's not what produces results. Financial records are like X-rays that allow a doctor to make a diagnosis. I leave the preparation to the skilled hands in maintaining data.

Q. How do you propose to compensate for your lack of experience?

Sample Ans.: I am a quick learner. Every time there is something new thrown at me, I take time to study it at the soonest time.

Q. What has disappointed you about work?

Sample Ans.: I once felt that I was not being given enough challenges to work on. I was a bit disappointed because I was so eager to go for more.

Q. Do your skills match this job or another job more closely?
Sample Ans.: I feel my skills are the best fit for this job.

Q. If you were hiring a manager for this job, what would you look for?
Sample Ans.: I would look into two essential things: the ability to do the job proper attitude to do it. Skills without the right attitude will not contribute to productive output.

Q. Do you have any serious medical issues that we should know?
Sample Ans.: I'm perfectly fit, and as of now, I haven't been diagnosed with any serious illness or medical condition. While the occasional fever and flu aren't strangers to me, I try to keep myself as fit and healthy as I can

Chapter 3

Management and Teamwork

Q. Do you prefer working as a member of a team or would you rather work alone?

Sample Ans.:   Whether I prefer to work as part of a team or alone depends on the best way to complete the job. While teamwork is very important, I can work just as hard alone. Either way, I would work equally hard with the initiative required for success.

Q. Do you work best alone or on a team?
Sample Ans.: I love the speed and energy of teamwork, and I also like concentrated time to work alone and execute on projects.

Q. Do you like to work with people?

Sample Ans.: Of course, I like to work with people. If we're to meet our goals and keep up with the growth that's predicted for this industry, we'll have to organize and coordinate the efforts of many people. There's a synergy in teamwork that can accomplish far more than the same individuals could work alone. When people work together, there's nothing like it. The energy and creativity they activate in each other are many times greater—the whole is greater than the sum of its parts.

Sample Ans.: I've always worked well with others, but I have no difficulty getting my work done independently. I'm a self-starter. I can set my goals, or I can take assigned goals and complete them. I'm comfortable with myself. If the job requires solitary hours like analyzing reports, crunching numbers, and making reports or presentations, I prefer to work alone so that I can focus on the job with concentration.

Q. Do you feel the only way to get a job done right is to do it yourself?

Sample Ans.: No, that kind of attitude results in mismanagement. If I am the only person in my group with a particular skill, my first priority after completing the task is to train someone else to do it in my absence. Effective team management requires that the job gets done even when some of the players are on the road, at a meeting, or on assignment elsewhere. I delegate responsibility but don't forget about it. If I have ultimate responsibility for something, I follow it up to make sure it is done. I'm a pilot, but I believe in a trained copilot and then in an automatic pilot, properly programmed, to keep us flying right on course.

Q. How would you feel about working for a female executive?

Sample Ans.: I'm an equal-opportunity employee. I enjoy working for anyone who practices good management and knows how to tap the potential of team members. Talent has no gender issue.

Q. How well do you cope with tension?

Sample Ans.: I've developed a program that works well for me. I eat properly, exercise regularly, and take vitamins. When work causes tension for whatever reason—deadlines, schedules, special projects, and unexpected obstacles, I'm ready I realize no stressful situation lasts forever, so I just set my sights high and keep climbing without looking down. I've already been there. Climbing is so much more fun when you realize what awaits you at the top.

Q Are you a team player?

Sample Ans.: Yes. While I will deny the fact that I can work independently with minimal supervision, I'm also one companion every leader would ever want to be in his team. Whatever task is assigned to me, I make sure it meets and exceeds what is expected of me. I also make it a point to reach out to teammates whenever needed.

Q. Do you consider yourself a team player?

Sample Ans.: Yes, I do consider myself an excellent team player. I've been lucky enough to work both as an individual contributor and as a part of the XYZ team in my present organization. So, I am fully aware of what each role demands of me. When given a task, I can handle it well with minimal supervision, and I can also work seamlessly within any team. As part of a team, I always keep communication lines open and am always ready to help my teammates wherever I can. know that collaboration is often the key to innovation and success, and I'm perfectly comfortable with working in a team environment.

Sample Ans.: Yes, I am. Right now, I'm working as an independent contributor to my present company. However, I've worked with my colleagues on numerous projects, and my transition into the team structure happens quite naturally. I like being a part of the team as it allows me to open up to new ideas and explore new avenues while working on different projects.

Q. What makes a good team player?

Sample Ans.: Being a good team player means being able to understand the goals of the team and be an active participant in reaching these goals. I have some experience of this, as I play weekly for my local basketball team. This has taught me the power of a harmonious team as well as how to deal with difficult people.

Q. Give me an example of a time when you worked on a team. What was your role?

Sample Ans.: In college, we have a team of six persons to organize events. While organizing activities with colleagues, my specific job was to facilitate members to arrive at a consensus plan and put it on paper.

Sample Ans.: In my last job, in our project, we had a team of 12 people all with soft skills. I was the team leader. I facilitated individual roles of the task to be done within the time frame. I established or tweaked processes or mediated conflict within the team.

Q. How have you gained commitment from your team?

Sample Ans.: I gain commitment from my teams by influencing and persuading them to set specific objectives and also buy into the process. Once they have established cooperation and cohesion, they are on board to attain the goal.

Q. How would you go about praising a team member in public?

Sample Ans.: I would use a time when we would be gathered in a group, such as a meeting to bring up the praise to the team member. I would recognize their success in front of the group so others could also learn best practices.

Q. How would you go about getting cohesion among a team who disagrees?

Sample Ans.: I would find common ground between the members who disagree. I would talk about the importance of the overall goal and the implications if we didn't come together to achieve it. We would then work together to come to an agreement that is a win/win for both sides.

Q. How do you set an example to those for your team members?

Sample Ans.: I will perform my best at everything and ensure that my actions match my words. My team sees that the expectations that are set for them are the same expectations I put on myself.

Q. How would you proceed to reorganize your team?

Sample Ans.: I would look at the overall goals of the organization and match my team's strengths with the reorganization.

Q. What was the most difficult decision for you to make?
Sample Ans.: It was a time when I had to choose between joining a group of employees protesting some issues in the company and staying away from the issue. I ended up being a mediator between the employees and our immediate supervisor, and I was glad.

Q. Who are the most important members of your team?

Sample Ans.: Everyone is equally important. Each person contributes something different to the team, and that makes us as a whole stronger.

Q. How do you deal with criticism?

Sample Ans.: I know that I'm not perfect. I'm still learning. Naturally, I make mistakes, but I feel that I can learn from my mistakes. I've always been enthusiastic about learning new things and acquiring new skills. If anyone offers me constructive feedback or criticism, I'll surely consider it and try to better myself. If you have a piece of advice for me that can benefit me and my work, I'll make sure to keep it with me moving forward.

Sample Ans.: Over the years in my professional experience, I've learned how to turn criticism into positive insights that I can use in my daily life. If ever I'm wrong and I'm criticized, I understand that I'm at fault. In such instances, I always try to rectify myself. I feel that I'm flexible and mature enough to handle criticism, both positive and negative.

Q. Would you rather be liked or feared?

Sample Ans.: Honestly, I would love to be well-liked and respected in my organization. For me, respect is necessary at my workplace. I would never like to be someone with whom my colleagues or my juniors cannot talk. I believe 'respected,' and not 'feared' is the right word here because being feared doesn't always command respect.

Q. How do you react to criticism by superiors if you believe it is unwarranted?

Sample Ans.: I've learned to think about the other person's comments for a while, so I can see them as feedback to my actions, not rejection of me. Why did the other individual see what I did as negative? Once I've taken time to think, I can respond, rather than merely react. If I still feel the criticism was unjust or was the result of some misunderstanding, I schedule a few minutes to sit down and talk it over calmly with my manager. I always try to present my case with a smile and without placing blame.

Q. Wouldn't you be better off in another company?

Sample Ans.: No, I'm sure I wouldn't. The type of opportunity and challenge I seek are here. Furthermore, my skills and experience match what you're looking for. I've researched my options thoroughly, and this company comes out on top for me. That's why I'm here.

Q. What is the most challenging thing about working with you?

Sample Ans.: My co-workers often say I'm too serious about my work. However, I have attended some personality-enhancing seminars to blend better with colleagues.

Q. How would a friend describe you?

Sample Ans.: Likeable, energetic, and an organizer who is always thinking of different ways to make being with friends fulfilling and enjoyable. Someone who keeps personal commitments protects personal confidences and makes the time to help the community. A family person whose house is in order.

Q. Will you be able to cope with a change in the work environment after working years in your last job?

Sample Ans.: Definitely, I welcome the challenge of learning about and adapting to a new environment. That's one of the reasons I'm seeking to make a change right now. I'd like to transfer all I've experienced to this company, while at the same time having the opportunity to meet new challenges and achieve new goals.

Q. As a manager, how would you go about establishing rapport with your staff?

Sample Ans.: I would first want to know as much about each individual as I could, professionally as well as personally. By reviewing each individual's position and work record, I would gain insight into his or her strong points and weaknesses. Similarly, by meeting with each person on a one-to-one basis and making myself open to candid dialogue, the stage would be set for a healthy working relationship.

Q. What makes the best manager?

Sample Ans.: The best manager is a person who is dedicated to company goals yet sensitive to the individuality of each employee he or she manages. Managing people effectively is a difficult job, but the rewards of helping them are great in contributing to company objectives. Exciting and igniting people is the manager's vision.

Q. What do your subordinates think are your strengths?

Sample Ans.: The people who have worked for me will tell you that I am fair and that I have a balanced approach to managing, one that considers both the business and people's side of every issue. They know I don't make hasty decisions that everyone will repent at leisure. And working for me usually means being on a winning team with a coach who expects everyone to give 110 per cent. I ask a lot, but they love it.

Q. What do your subordinates think are your weaknesses?

Sample Ans.: What might be perceived by some as weaknesses are my strengths. I expect a lot from my staff, but no more than I expect from myself. I look for and reward people who show initiative and creativity. People I've supervised in the past will tell you that they worked harder in my department than in any other job. They'll also tell you they enjoyed it more because they were accomplishing more.

Q. What plan of action do you take when facing a problem?

Sample Ans.: Before I act, I think. I try to distance myself from the problem so I can look at it objectively and analyze all sides. Sometimes; I even write it down to see it more clearly. When I've reached a decision, I present my planned solution to the people affected by it or to those who must carry it out. I get their input, incorporate any appropriate suggestions, and then we implement the plan. I believe in immediate but realistic solutions to problems. Ignoring them rarely makes them go away.

Q. What suggestion/s have you made in your previous employment that was implemented?

Sample Ans.: I once suggested that management and staff should have more regular meetings instead of quarterly meetings. I was happy that the administration took note of this and even commended me for taking a good initiative

Chapter 4

Aptitude Questions

Q. Describe your management philosophy.

Sample Ans.: More than anything else, I think that management is getting things done through other people. The manager's job is to provide the resources and environment in which people can work effectively. I try to do this by creating teams, judging people solely based on their performance, distributing work fairly, and empowering workers, to the extent possible, to make their own decisions. I've found that this breeds loyalty and inspires hard work.

Q. What does "success" mean to you?

Sample Ans.: Success means working with others to come up with efficient designs that can be up on the assembly line quickly. Of course, the financial rewards of managing a department give me the means to travel during my vacations. That's the thing I love most in my personal life.

Q. What does "failure" mean to you?

Sample Ans.: Failure is not getting the job done when I have the means to do so. For example, once I was faced with a huge project. I should have realized at the outset that I didn't have the time. I must have been thinking there were 48 hours in a day! I also didn't have the knowledge I needed to do it correctly. Instead of asking some of the other people in my department for help, I blundered through. That won't ever happen to me again if I can help it!"

Q. What extracurricular activities were you involved in?

Sample Ans.: I wish I'd had more time to write for the school paper. Whenever I wasn't studying, I pretty much had to work to pay for college. But I learned several things from the jobs I held that most people learn only after they've been in their careers for a while—such as how to work with other people and how to manage my time effectively."

Q. Tell me about the types of people you have trouble getting along with.

Sample Ans.: I'm too impatient with slow performers. I don't expect to ever accept poor workers, but I'm learning to be more patient as the world is filled with 'C,' rather than 'A' or 'B' people "

Q. Do you manage your time well?

Sample Ans.: I rarely miss a deadline. When circumstances beyond my control interfere, I make up for the time lost as quickly as possible. I establish a To-Do list first thing in the morning. Then I add to it—and reprioritize tasks, if necessary—as the day goes on.

Q. How do you handle change?

Sample Ans.: Recently, my boss decided our company needed to develop a virtual storefront on the World Wide Web. I was given the task, along with a designer, of taking the project from the research phase to operation in eight weeks. I didn't have any special expertise in the area of computers and online communications, so I have to assume I was given the task because I adapt well.

Q. If you could start your career over again, what would you do differently?

Sample Ans.: My only regret is that I didn't go in this direction sooner. I started my career in editorial, and I enjoyed that. But once I got into marketing, I found I loved it. Now, I can't wait to get to work every day.

Q. How do you generally handle conflict?

Sample Ans.: I'm usually able to work things out or anticipate problems before they occur. When conflicts can't be avoided, I don't back down. But I certainly do try to be reasonable.

Sample Ans.: I've had confrontations with co-workers who weren't holding up their end of a job. I feel that employees owe it to their bosses, customers, and co-workers to do their jobs properly.

Q. How do you behave when you have a problem with a co-worker?

Sample Ans.: I had to work with a designer who was obstinate about listening to any of my suggestions. He would answer me in monosyllables and then drag his feet before doing anything I requested. Finally, I said, 'Look, we're both professionals. Neither of us has the right answer all the time. I have noticed that you don't like my suggestions. But rather than resist implementing them, why don't we just discuss what you don't like?' That worked like a charm. We eventually became friends.

Q. Was there anything your company (or department or team) could have done to be more successful?

Sample Ans.: Sure, we could have expanded our product line, perhaps even doubled it, to take advantage of our superior distribution. But we just didn't have the capital and couldn't get the financing.

Q. Have you been in charge of budgeting, approving expenses, and monitoring departmental progress against financial goals? Are you very qualified in this area?

Sample Ans.: Well, I've never actually run a department, but I've had to set and meet budgetary goals for several projects I've worked on. I did this so often that I took a class to learn how to set up and use Microsoft Excel spreadsheets.

Q. Why are you thinking of leaving your current job?

Sample Ans.: There is a great deal I enjoy about my current job. However my potential for growth in this area is limited at Closely Held, Inc., because of the size of the company and the fact that expansion is not a part of its current strategic plan.

Q. Why haven't you received any offers so far?

Tips: It's important to tell the truth, however, because the interviewer's next logical question may follow.

Sample Ans.: I have had an offer. But the situation was not right for me. I'm especially glad that I didn't accept because I now have a shot at landing this position.

Q. If you have these complaints about your current job/boss/company, and they think so highly of you, why haven't you brought your concerns to their attention?

Sample Ans.: Grin & Bear It is aware of my desire to move up. But the company is still small. There's not much they can do about it. The management team is terrific. There's no need right now to add to it, and they are aware of some of the problems this creates in keeping good performers. It's something they talk about quite openly.

Q. What made you get into technical support?

Sample Ans.: I decided to go into technical support because I've been fascinated by technology all my life, and I also love working with people. I want to use my technical know-how to directly solve issues customers are having. I want to be the person that makes life easier and more enjoyable for folks who've run into a problem.

Q. Describe a time when you went above and beyond to help a customer.

Sample Ans.: At my previous company, I remember one customer had an issue that kept happening. The common fixes we were using were only temporarily solving the problem. After doing a bit of research, I was able to design and develop a new solution. I called the customer personally and implemented the repair."

Q. Is technical knowledge or customer service more important?

Sample Ans.: First, let me say that customer service skills are very important. You must be able to empathize with people and address their needs. Good communication is crucial. With that said, I have a technical background, and I understand the amount of knowledge you need to solve issues. Technical skills are more important because, without in-depth knowledge of the hardware and software, you won't be able to efficiently do your job.

Q. Where do you see yourself in five years?

Sample Ans.: In this position, I plan to add skills and experience. Honestly, I would like to move into a management role in technical support within five years. What I like about this company is how they actively develop employees. I feel like I can consistently improve here and move into bigger roles for your organization.

Q. What are the two things you would like to improve about yourself?

Sample Ans.: The two things I would like to improve on over the next two years are my supervisory and computer skills. I already know supervision and compilers well, but I would like to do even better. I'm going to take some special courses to help me improve in these areas.

Q. What are some of the reasons for your success?

Sample Ans.: I attribute much of my success to one of my college mentors, who instilled in me a particular attitude about work and life in general. He stressed the importance of being both competent and tenacious. I've always tried to improve my skills either on the job or through special training programs. I approach work with enthusiasm and stick with it until it's done, however difficult and challenging it may be. I don't have time to find excuses for not doing something or pushing work to others. I think this particular stick-to-it attitude has served me well. And I try to instill a similar attitude in others I work with. I think success comes to those who know
what they want to do, where they are going, and put in the necessity effort to see that things get accomplished.

Q. What duties in your present/most recent job do you find it difficult to do?

Tips: Try to identify things that either are not part of the job description of the job you are interviewing for or that are a minor or unimportant part of the job.

Sample Ans.:
With so many orders being shipped I sometimes find it difficult to keep up with filing after the shipping commotions.

Q. Describe your typical workday.

Sample Ans.: My typical day involves a great deal of accounting work and meetings with the chief financial officer and bookkeeper. I usually begin by balancing the ledger and reporting yesterday's balance to the chief financial officer. I meet with the bookkeeper to make sure all invoices have been posted and payments have been issued. The remainder of my day involves meetings with other financial officers to resolve any problems arising in the daily accounting process. I would say I'm involved in managing our financial team and doing a great deal of troubleshooting throughout
the day.

Q. Do you ever lose your temper?

Sample Ans.: I sometimes get irritated but I generally don't lose my temper. I've learned to separate my temperament on the job.

Q. How do you deal with stressful situations?

Sample Ans.: Over the years, I've learned to put stressful situations in a better perspective than I used to. I know some stress comes with the job. If the stress involves the work of my subordinates, I usually open up lines of communication with them to with any issues contributing to the stress. If the stress is a result of the daily workload, I get through the day knowing l well my exercise routine at the end of the day will renew me both physically & and mentally. I've also given up coffee, which seems to contribute to stress, and I've joined a health club.

Q. How well do you work under deadlines?

Sample Ans.: While others may have difficulty managing deadlines, including experiencing a great deal and stress, I do well under stress. I tend to take charge, organize tasks, and move everything along quickly to get the job done. More importantly, I try to avoid doing things only at the deadline time. My goal is to get tasks done well in advance so that we have spare time to do the necessary evaluation required for producing a high-quality product.

Q. How do you feel about the contributions you made to XYZ corporation?

Sample Ans.: I feel good about what I accomplished there. When I arrived, the division was in disarray. Morale was low, employee turnover was high, and performance was at best questionable. Within five months I managed to turn this situation around by implementing a new management system that gave employees greater say in what they were doing. Morale increased dramatically, employee turnover declined by 30 per cent, and our division became one of the best performers in the organization.

We also became the model for management changes that eventually
took place in all other divisions. I think the organization as a whole performs much better today than ever before.

Q. What do you wish you had accomplished in your present/most recent job but were unable to?

Sample Ans.: My goal was to cut customer complaints by 50%. In the past three months, we've cut complaints by 40%. I think given another month we could reach the 50% mark.

Q. What skills would you say are most important for an engineer?

Sample Ans.: The ability to be innovative is the most important quality for an engineer. We have to be able to look at things in a new way, even if it means realizing our past ideas are not as perfect as we thought they were. Our job is always trying to top our last design. Being a good communicator is also a good skill because you have to be able to explain your idea to the rest of your team and get them to buy into it.

Q. How would you explain a car's wheel and axle system to a layperson?

Sample Ans.: Axles serve two main purposes. They help bear some of the weight of the car, and they help the steering system turn your wheels. So, when you turn your steering wheel to the right, the axle helps turn the tyres and absorbs any weight shift.

Q. What is a new engineering skill you've acquired in the last year?

Sample Ans.: I took a course on the design of solar water heating systems a few months ago. As the future of energy moves toward solar, I wanted to be familiar with the components and processes of using solar collector systems to generate energy. A lot of what

I learned can be applied to other forms of solar absorption construction.

Q. How do you keep from getting bored when doing routine engineering work?

Sample Ans.: Well, there are always countless possibilities about how to create. One of the best parts of my job is that I get to use tried and true components but assemble them in a new way. I avoid boredom at work by looking for new and improved ways to use the same parts more efficiently. Even when that's not a part of my professional role, I can get that out of my system at home by tinkering on my car or building things in my garage.

Chapter 5

Leadership

Q. What are the most important values you demonstrate as a leader?

Sample Ans.:   The most important value that I have is my integrity. I demonstrate honesty and trust in all my actions to establish credibility as a leader. By having this conviction behind my words and actions, those who I lead are gain-bought into the direction I take them.

Q. How do you get others to accept your ideas?

Sample Ans.:   I talk about the benefits of the idea and how to apply it. I would stay open to other thoughts and change my ideas in a way that we can all agree. When you gain buy-in from others, you are much more successful in attaining the goals than when you make it mandatory to follow the procedure.

Q. Describe a time you took a leadership position when you did not have the title of a leader.

Sample Ans.:   In college, we were put into groups of four to complete a marketing project. We had to prepare a 15-page paper and a 10-minute presentation on a new product. We want to introduce that outside the U.S. I took the initiative among the group to lead a discussion on how we should split up the work when we meet throughout the semester and deadlines for each person's part of the work. Because I was the one to take the lead in the discussion and had a plan in mind, I gained the buy-in of the other members quickly. I took everyone's e-mail address and created a group email to help us all keep track of our progress so we could help each other outside of class and our meetings. By the end of the semester, my group achieved a 95% on our project.

Q. What sort of leader would your team say that you are?

Sample Ans.: They would describe me as someone who will clear the way when there are obstacles and always has their back.

Q. What is the most difficult part of being a leader?

Sample Ans.: In some ways, although you are part of a group, you are alone. It's a leader's responsibility to see the end goal and vision of an organization to lead others towards it. When others do not see it the same way, you have to be the lone voice to bring them back on track.

Q. How do you measure success for you as a leader?

Sample Ans.: By the goals that the team achieves. When someone on the team is successful, then it reflects on my leadership.

Q. What motivates you to be a leader?

Sample Ans.: I am motivated by my team's growth and achievement of their professional and personal goals.

Q. What is a leader's best asset?

Sample Ans.: Their ability to motivate and inspire a team of professionals who can work together to achieve the goals of the organization.

Q. Are you more comfortable with verbal or written communication?

Sample Ans.: I am comfortable with both types of communication. However, I feel that verbal communication is more effective.

Q. How do you go about resolving conflict?

Sample Ans.: I take a mediated approach to conflict. I believe it's important to listen to both sides and understand where each is coming from. There is usually some common ground between conflict, and I start there and build.

Q. Give an example of how did you a handle a time when you had to make an unpopular decision?

Sample Ans.: Last year I decided to change our commission structure to our sales reps. I felt it was a necessary change because there were too many sales reps who were doing the bare minimum to collect a pay check. Needless to say, many of the sales reps were upset with the decision. I reiterated the reasons for the change and ensured they had the tools they needed to be successful in the new commission structure. The organization saw an increase in their revenue and sales reps were making 5% more with the new commission structure.

Q. How do you organize projects and tasks?

Sample Ans.: I organize them by what is the most important and time-sensitive to complete.

Q. Explain a time when you were not able to meet a deadline?

Sample Ans.: There was a big project that my team was working on, and I had split up the work among some members and myself. During that time, one member of the team had to leave due to their spouse getting a position in another city. He left at a critical time, and I had to re-assign his duties to someone else. I make the new person work to speed with the progression of the project and due to this, was not able to complete it on time. We were still able to complete the project a few days after the deadline even with the change in the team member.

Q. Have you ever taken on a job that you were unqualified for?

Sample Ans.: I took on management responsibilities in my previous position to take the place of my manager who had left. I did not have any management experience, but I knew that the team was not going to be able to be effective without a leader in place. I may have made a few mistakes, but ultimately was successful in taking on that additional responsibility. The upper-level management was impressed by my growth and efforts, so they ended up promoting me into that position.

Q. What leadership skills do you find most useful?

Sample Ans.:   It's lead by example. In my last position, we created a new dress code policy, and I was asked to enforce it as the supervisor. My approach was to discuss the new policy, clearly outline what new clothing items were acceptable and provide a deadline for when the policy went into full effect. I also listened to any concerns my team had about whether the new dress code would be comfortable enough to work in. At the next shift, I wore the new uniform to show my team what the appropriate dress code looked like and to demonstrate how it was more comfortable than the old uniform. As a result, my team felt more confident switching to the new policy, and the whole team began following the dress code before the deadline.

Q. How do you make sure projects and tasks stay on schedule?

Sample Ans.: When my team is assigned a collaborative project, I always begin by discussing the project's objective and purpose. Then, I assign each team member individual tasks and deadlines. I find that when the team knows the goals of the overall project, they can better see how their role impacts the project's success. When we work on a project, I hold full team meetings to allow individual team members to share their progress. I try to celebrate the team's hard work to keep them motivated. I also check with each team member to see their progress, address any risks or deadline issues and provide additional clarity. Checking in outside of the group meeting can make team members feel more comfortable sharing if they need extra help. I find that the process of remaining available to my team and encouraging their success allows them to stay focused and feel supported.

Q. How do you handle disagreements on your team?

Sample Ans.: My goal is to facilitate discussion and help my team find compromise when there is a disagreement. In my last role, two of my team members had different approaches to completing their part of the project. I let each side explain what their thought process was and what benefits they saw in their method. I encouraged respectful discussion and positive commentary. After each side outlined their arguments, I helped them brainstorm the ways in which both arguments could become a combined solution. This process enabled the team members to work together and see each other's perspectives. It also helped them remember that they both were working toward the same goal and should collaborate on the best way to complete their tasks.

Q. What was a difficult decision you made as a leader?

Sample Ans.: I once had the option to give my team a long holiday weekend. I knew how hard my team was working, but we had an important project that we needed to finish by Monday. My first thought was to give them the long weekend to rest, but we would have had to rush to complete the work. This decision risked impacting productivity and the quality of our work. I then thought of not giving them the long weekend and encouraging them to keep working on schedule. This option would avoid pressuring them to rush but also risked them feeling overworked or underappreciated. I ultimately decided not to grant the long weekend and emphasized the importance of completing the project. On that Friday, I ordered a catered lunch and offered to let them take a long weekend next week to thank them. I think this compromise showed that I cared about my team's well-being but also valued their reputation for providing quality work on time."

Q. Can you describe a leadership challenge you overcame?

Sample Ans.: During one of my team's recent projects, we were approaching the deadline but were not making the progress we needed to meet our goal. Many team members were feeling overwhelmed, and the pressure was affecting their work quality. I took on a number of tasks and worked alongside them to meet the deadline. My team felt supported knowing I was taking on additional responsibilities so they did not have to compromise the quality of their work. We completed the project on time, and the client was pleased with our results. After reviewing the project's initial planning process, I realized that our timeline and workload were not realistic. In the future, I will spend more time analysing the initial planning process and discussing realistic expectations. I want to make sure my team stays motivated, so spending more time before beginning the project can help me better delegate tasks.

Q. Can you tell me about a time when you demonstrated leadership capabilities on the job?

Sample Ans.: While I was working for my last employer, I was given a special project to oversee. Ensuring the project was a success was my responsibility, so I knew I had to step up. Along with coordinating the work of a diverse team, I set up weekly strategy meetings to keep everything on target. I delegated tasks, set the timeline, and followed up regularly to ensure everyone was achieving their goals. Additionally, I coached team members who fell behind, preventing small challenges from derailing the project. Ultimately, we finished on time, and every deliverable met or exceeded expectations.

Q. Which supporting skills do you think are most important when it comes to leadership?

Sample Ans.: In the world of leadership, you can't ignore the power of active listening and communication skills. Ensuring team members feel heard makes a difference. Along with being a sign of respect, active listening demonstrates that I value their perspective, which is essential. Couple that with clear communication, and you increase the team's odds of success.

Q. When there is a disagreement on your team, how do you handle it?

Sample Ans.: If I notice signs of conflict on a team, the first step I take is to schedule one-on-one meetings with each person. That allows me to create a safe space and get their perspective on the matter, ensuring everyone feels they can speak freely. Along the way, I ask probing questions to get additional clarity. Once I have a solid understanding, I work to find resolutions, relying on a calm, metered, collaborative approach involving all parties that leads to a suitable compromise. That way, everyone feels valued, respected, and involved, leading to better outcomes."

Q. Tell me about your approach to delegation.

Sample Ans.: I view delegation as a critical part of the broader success equation. When I have tasks to divvy out, I use a two-fold approach. First, I consider which team members either have the needed skills or could acquire valuable skills by taking on the duty. Next, I examine workloads to determine if other adjustments are necessary to make handling that responsibility manageable. Once I have a preferred team member in mind, I meet with them to discuss the task. Along with outlining what's required, I discuss expectations. Additionally, I ask if there's anything in their current workload that would prevent them from meeting those expectations. By using that approach, I can clarify the requirements without accidentally overburdening a team member. Plus, it allows me to address any questions they may have, allowing them to get started on the right foot.

Q. What do you think is most important in creating a positive culture?

Sample Ans.: In my opinion, the most important factor when you want to create a positive culture is recognition. Ideally, gratitude shouldn't just come from managers but from every level of the department. Everyone likes to feel valued and appreciated for their efforts, so it has a positive impact on morale. Plus, it encourages beneficial behaviours while creating a culture of respect. Together, that creates an enthusiastic environment where positive mindsets are common, leading to better results overall."

Q. What is the motivation for your leadership? As a leader how will you measure your success?

Sample Ans.: A Leader gets motivated by his/her team's achievements like team-mates finishing their targets, achieving their professional as well as personal goals, etc. A leader's success lies in his/her team member's success.

Q. When you come across any bad news then how will you put it in front of your team?

Sample Ans.: To deliver any bad news to the team, the best way is to arrange a small meeting with the team and deliver it. I will try to explain all the possible solutions that need to be implemented shortly so that such mistakes cannot take place. At last, I will ask my team to share their views, ideas, concerns or any suggestions that can be carried out in the next activity to avoid such situations.

Q. What is your approach when you are not clear about achieving your goals on time?

Sample Ans.: As a leader, I should be ready to accept any comments or opinions from your team. And should not hesitate to seek help from your immediate superiors or your team-mates. Taking all the inputs into account, I should come up with a new and clear agenda on how to finish your target on time.

Q. How will you encourage your team by sharing the other team member's success?

Sample Ans.: Praising one's success in front of others will inspire and motivate them to work harder. It encourages and gives confidence to others to perform better. One who succeeds in their career should be rewarded. As a leader, if we link the performance of a team member to any reward or recognition, then it motivates them to work harder.

Q. Is there any strong or unique skill in you that makes me hire you?

Sample Ans.: My career objective is to serve a professionally managed company and achieve a challenging position by utilizing my abilities developed through my experience and education and contributing to enhancing the goals of the company. This makes you hire me into your organization.

Q. What is over-supervision in your view as a leader? How will it affect an employee?

Sample Ans.: Over supervision is nothing but when a person is given more direction than what he needs. When an employee is under such a situation, they get frustrated and angry. They stop trying and taking risks. They stop making decisions on their own, and their participation and initiation come down.

Scenario-Based Questions

Scenario: You have asked one of your team members to prepare a report for a newly added requirement to your current project. Usually, he completes the task assigned to him on time with encouragement from you. However, this time his report is overdue.

Q. How would you handle this situation?

Sample Ans.: I will tell him or her what you are expecting from him and when you want the report to be completed. But discuss with him regarding the reason for not preparing the report on time. Apart from that, you need to keep track of his performance daily.

Scenario: Recently, you have been facing a problem with one of your team members. He became lazy and exhausted. Your constant follow-up has brought task completion. Because of such experience with him, you suspect that he is not capable of completing a high-priority task.

Q. How will you overcome such a situation?

Sample Ans.: As a leader, I will involve him in Problem-Solving with the task and offer support to him. And will try to utilize his ideal in the task completion. Apart from this, I will try to draw out his attitude and feelings concerning this task assignment.

Scenario: One of your senior employees is assigned a new job which is important to your team shortly. Even though he is excited about the new job, he has no experience with the task.

Q. How will you motivate him to take up the task and proceed further?

Sample Ans.:   I will discuss the job with him by defining the necessary activities to proceed with it, supporting his ability to do the task. And also highlight his outstanding performance in the past. Ask him to share his views on the new job so that they can be implemented.

Scenario: A highly productive and efficient member of your team has asked for your help on a task. He is familiar with working effectively on his own but some work hurdles have discouraged him from solving the task by himself.

Q. How will you solve his problem and make him comfortable to work?

Sample Ans.: I will try to analyse the problems and outline the methods to solve them. Finally, I will help him to determine and implement an appropriate solution to resolve the task on his own.

Scenario: A new employee has been assigned to your team to perform a new assignment. He is excited and confident enough to accept the task but he has no experience in that job or task.

Q. How will you deal with that new employee?

Sample Ans.: First of all, I will welcome him into the team and explain to him all the details regarding the new task and will tell him what the job demands from him. A leader will guide him on how to proceed with the task. I will also convey to him what is the expectation and will monitor his work frequently and closely.

Scenario: Recently you have been appointed as head of a department. Under the former HOD's supervision, the team functioned satisfactorily with his encouragement and support. Since you have taken the authority, the team's performance has come down.

Q. Will you identify their problem and suggest a solution for it?

Sample Ans.: Immediately, I will call for a team meeting and conduct a discussion regarding the team's low performance and will suggest possible solutions to overcome those difficulties. I will also support their efforts to indicate any corrective actions. At last, will ask for any input and suggestions from the team.

Chapter 6
Why You Should Be Hired?

Q. Why do you want to work for us?

Sample Ans.1. I was tremendously excited when I saw your advertised position. I know your company well, as I already use some of the great services you offer. I believe that I can contribute significantly to the continuing growth and success of your company.

Sample Ans.2. I would be proud to work for a company like yours with such a long history of leadership in the industry. I have carried out web research and believe that the company's XYZ products and its future projections are very impressive and promising. The XXX team is the team I would take pride to work with. A place where my skills or background fits perfectly and can be utilized, respectively.

Sample Ans.3. Your company made its fortune in making great products that help people do X. But on top of that, it is the kind of place where I can fit in and excel, so I was thrilled to see you have this opening. Your company believes in providing superior service, and I share the same values. It enables me to not only fit into your organization but complement the team as well.

Sample Ans.4. I was delighted to see on your website that your featured employees are talking about how great it is to work for your company. These days so many people seem to despise where they work for one reason or another. It's wonderful to see that your employees are proud to talk about how much they love their jobs.

Sample Ans.5. This company is on the list of most admired companies every year. I want to play a role in ensuring this company stays on that list. I want to be part of a company that offers no less than quality in terms of products and after-sales services

Sample Ans6. I chose this job profile and your company because I feel it's a perfect match for my skills and experience. Presently, this is exactly the kind of role that I can visualize myself in as it aligns well with my career goals. I think with my skill set and background, and your guidance, I can grow to be a valuable asset to your company.

Q. Why did you apply to our company?

Sample Ans.: I applied to your company because your team is making life easier and more enjoyable for millions of people. The scale of your work is tremendous, and I feel like my work here can have a real positive impact. I also love the company culture and how there's a focus on teamwork and collaboration.

Q. Where do you predict that this industry is going in the next three years?

 Sample Ans.: I think that we're going to see this industry rapidly taking off. In my view, it is quickly evolving into the perfect 24/7 business and profit centre. It's already expanding and connecting customers. At that point, you'll be able to be recognized among top best-performing companies in the country in these business segments.

Q. How does the fact that you are a recent college graduate benefit our company?

Sample Ans.: I'm anxious to get started using all I've learned. I'm already trained in new methods and procedures, so I should be able to implement them immediately. My college education was a very full-time packed schedule of activities including special projects. In addition, I had a part-time job to help support myself. I worked constantly. I had to make every hour count, so I became adept at time management and planning. No one supervises you in college. You know whether you've been successful when your grades are issued. There are long periods between evaluations, so you must be self-disciplined and budget your time. I have the latest training and skills and the willingness to get the job done.

Q. What makes you qualified for this job?

Sample Ans.: I feel that I'm qualified because I have a bachelor's degree in computer science. I have advanced skills with customer support tools like Zendesk. Also, I have five years of experience as a technical support specialist in the software industry. I know your company operates on a global scale, and I can provide support in both English and Spanish.

Q. What do you believe are your special qualifications for this job?

Sample Ans.: (Tips: Begin by mentioning any specific training and experience that apply to the position. Then, I have direct insight into the requirements of this job and know how to increase efficiency/productivity/sales/etc. There are a great many challenges to be met, and the right person—someone who approaches them with energy and determination—will achieve results greater than anyone thought possible. I believe I'm the right person.)

Q. Do you think you are overqualified
    for this job role?

Sample Ans.: No, I don't think I am overqualified for this job role, but I think I'm perfectly qualified for it. I have the right skill set, educational background, and experience for this post, and I believe I can use them to my advantage at your company, that is if I'm hired. I feel that there's no end to learning. So, yes, I'm well qualified for this post.

Q. Why do you think you are a good fit for this role?

Sample Ans.: It would be a privilege to be associated with your company, which boasts a long-standing history in thought leadership. I've done my homework, and I know what the company stands for, I feel that your vision perfectly aligns with my beliefs. I would very much like to be a part of your X team because this is where my skills and knowledge will be best utilized.

Q. Why should we consider hiring you?

Sample Ans.:   your advert said that you were looking for someone who is highly numerate, has good teamwork and presentation skills, and a willingness to work hard. I hope that my experience as a financial analyst at Transworld Bank shows that I'm good with numbers. Both of the jobs I've held so far have required me to work often long hours in a close-knit team and it's something that I very much enjoy. And my boss singled out my presentation

Sample Ans.: You need a self-starter who can handle a large territory and deal regularly with a variety of people—from hospital purchasing agents and directors of nursing to private physicians. You need someone who can take objectives and systematically meet them using creative approaches. My qualification gives me the scientific knowledge to understand the technical aspects of this product line and to discuss it intelligently with physicians and other healthcare professionals. I've proven my ability to work with people and numbers and to handle big responsibilities with a minimum of supervision. In my previous sales work, I usually exceeded my quotas. To sum up, my ability, experience, skill, and personality match the requirements and diverse responsibilities of the position.

Sample Ans.: In my XXX years of experience as a manager, I have built-up solid motivational and team-working skills. I was awarded twice as the manager of the year for my excellent methodologies for motivating employees to encounter challenges and meet deadlines. If hired, I will carry forward this ability of leadership and strategies to achieve profit gains for this company.

Sample Ans.: The subjects I chose while working for my degree in XXX subject has prepared me for this particular post. Also, my two-year experience working with company X has given me the platform to master the skills that I needed to deliver for this position. It seems as if I was prepared all my life to land this job.

Sample Ans.: For this particular job, I have the perfect combination of skills and experience that is required. I also bring rich experience of strong analytical and problem-solving skills that I have gained while working with other companies. My dedication to excellent work standards will add value to the team and the company.

Sample Ans.: I am quite aware of the company's mission of acquiring the largest consumer base in the area to become the front-runner in the supplier's or provider's community. My domain knowledge and hold over the customer base can make a big contribution towards this. I would enjoy the challenge of growing this business bigger.

Sample Ans.: My years of experience in this field is something that can truly contribute to this company's success. My sense of dedication in every task that I handle is a big plus. I believe my skills and work attitude measure up to your company's standards.

Q. What sets you apart from other candidates?
Sample Ans.:

Sample Ans.: I'm sure that this profile has attracted many candidates with impressive profiles. However, since I'm not familiar with what other candidates have to bring to the table, I'll not compare myself to others. As for myself, I am a creative individual with excellent organizational and problem-solving skills. I'm also a diligent and dedicated professional, and I think these qualities make me a strong contender for this position."

Q. What experience do you have in this field?

Sample Ans.: I have created several systems that are still in use to this day. Some of the systems I'm proud which include [mention those remarkable ones]

Q. How would you be an asset to our company?

Sample Ans.: I believe I have the essential qualities that match your company's job profile. This is the reason I want to become a part of your organization. I have always been a goal and result-oriented person, and I know that whatever responsibilities come my way, I will see them through. If I get the space and push to grow and develop as a professional, I will repay it with fierce loyalty and dedication.

Sample Ans.: As a fresher, I've not been exposed to the work environment yet. But I know that given the right platform and mentorship, I can prove my mettle and drive tangible results for the organization. I'm headstrong, and practical, and possess excellent people skills. If given a chance, I'll be ready to expose myself to different challenges, roles, and working conditions. So, I think, in a short time, I'll be able to grow into a valuable asset for your company.

Sample Ans.: My skills in [key skill for the position] are outstanding. I have earned a lot of awards and certifications from my past employers. As an employee, I handle pressure with ease and can work with minimal supervision.

Q. Let's say that I offer you a job. Please tell me how the company will benefit. / In what specific ways will our company benefit from hiring you?

Sample Ans.: I am an LED sign expert. I have been selling huge, LED signs to for the past five years. Your company will benefit from my expertise on three counts: First; I will train your sales staff how to close deals more quickly and profitably. Second; I will share my extensive contact base with your company. Third; I will reorganize your service department to be more "hands-on." Then, your customers will give your company those glowing referrals that will lead to even more new business.

Sample Ans.: The company will be adding to their workforce an employee whose skills and training most closely match the job requirements. Further, it will be getting the benefit his experience. My background relates directly to the position being considered and is a primary reason why it will take me less time to produce or deliver. I'm dedicated and learn quickly. I try always to excel at what I do. So, when you hire me, there's little risk you'll be interviewing for the job again soon.

Q. If needed, would you be willing to relocate for this job?

Sample Ans.: I would certainly like to travel if the opportunity presents itself and is rewarding for my career at your company. I think work-related travels are excellent for exploring new places, new business opportunities, and connecting with people from diverse backgrounds.

Sample Ans.: Yes, I would be willing to travel/relocate to new locations. I love travelling, and I think going to new places will be a delightful experience for me.

Q. Would you be in a position to work overtime if required? How do you feel about working overtime or at odd hours?

Sample Ans.: Absolutely; a job is a lot more than a paycheck— it's a responsibility, a task to complete, even if it requires that I work overtime. Whether I'm compensated for overtime or not, I derive personal satisfaction from the extra effort that results in success. Extra effort makes the difference between a good job and a better one.

Sample Ans.: I understand that being asked to work for an extended number of hours comes with a good reason in the first place, so I'm ok with it. It is an extra effort that means something for the company. I'll be happy to do it.

Sample Ans.: If I'm required to put in extra hours to complete urgent deliverables, or if there's a resource crunch in the team, I'll be willing to put in overtime for my team and organization. I am always willing to contribute to my team in any way possible, including working extra hours and odd times. However, I do expect to get comp offs to unwind and get back on track for what's ahead of me.

Sample Ans.: In my current position, my job is set within the 9-6 routine. However, I never back off from putting in extra effort and time if the need arises. If I've to work odd shifts and extra hours to achieve something for myself and my company, I am willing to do it, provided I get compensatory time off afterwards.

Q. Do any of your friends or relatives work for this company?
Sample Ans.: No. I found your ads on a popular job posting website. *(Tips. If your research suggests that this company likes as policy, hiring friends and relatives of employees, even for unrelated positions, then you may mention affirmatively. Be sure not to misrepresent references.)*

Q. Have you ever worked in a job that you hated?

Sample Ans.: Not exactly hated. I once had a job that did not exactly match my qualifications. Nevertheless, I was glad I took the job because it was an opportunity to learn something new and add to my list of experiences.

Q. What would you rate yourself on a scale of 1 to 10?

Sample Ans.: A score of 8/10 is more reasonable. Go on to say something like: "I believe that I'm very good at X, but there is always more to learn.

Sample Ans.: On a scale of 1 to 10, I will rate myself an 8. There's always room for improvement and upskilling.

Q. What have been the biggest frustrations in your career?

Sample Ans.: I've always approached my career with enthusiasm, so I haven't experienced much frustration. However, when I find myself up against a source of annoyance, I convert it into an opportunity to prove myself and set an example for others to follow. It has worked very well for them and me because enthusiasm is contagious.

Q. What have been the biggest failures in your career?

Sample Ans.: While I honestly can't recall any major failures, I've had a few temporary setbacks—mainly when I tried to do too much at once.

Q. What risks did you take in your previous job and what were the outcome?

Sample Ans.: In my previous job, it appeared that the only way to succeed was to drive myself and those around me to the limit of our potential. My risks have always been carefully considered. I took them only after making sure I could save my employer money or time by my action. I put careful thought into my decisions, the outcome was consistently positive, and my success was noticed. By the time I left, I had the reputation of being an innovator who knew how to get the job done.

Q. How did you like working for your (current/previous) boss?

Sample Ans.: Working for my boss has been a great experience. He / She is a dedicated professional who understands the business and how to be successful in it. As a result, he/she has earned the loyalty and respect of the entire department, and I will be leaving/left with mixed emotions. From the time I began working at GECO (the name of the company), my supervisor took a sincere interest in my work. Under (his/her) guidance, I grew personally and professionally. I've learned that a congenial working environment is a collective responsibility. All employees have to work together and respect each other for the job to get done. I've been fortunate to work with and learn from someone who trusted and believed in (his/her) subordinates. That trust gave me the confidence I needed to be successful. I plan to use the same leadership style when I supervise others.

Q. What was your biggest challenge with your previous boss?

Sample Ans.: My previous boss was very strict when it came to deadlines and output. It was a challenge for me to meet every expectation he made. It was also a good learning experience for me because it only made me better at what I do.

Q. What have you done to improve your knowledge in the last year?

Sample Ans.: I have attended several self-improvements, time management, and personality development seminars. I have also participated in training workshops related to [industry].

Q. In the past year, what steps have you taken toward upskilling?

115. Sample Ans.: Last year, I attended various seminars for professional grooming and personality development. Also, I took

two courses relevant to my field of work and attended training workshops conducted by my present employer.

Q. How would you define your success?

Sample Ans.:   I would define my success as I have learned through the years and use it when circumstances arise or demand. To me, success is not just my achievements but also the efforts of the people around me. I would define success at work as what I have learned from key job assignments and experiences. I believe that greater success can be achieved while working as a team towards a common goal. I believe the new position I am applying for will enable me to reach higher and be more successful

Q. How do you respond to change?

Sample Ans.: A couple of people left our team in the space of just a week, which meant that we were heavily understaffed for over a month. The rest of the team had to readjust our shifts to ensure that the helpdesk remained manned at all times. I volunteered for a few additional shifts because I knew that our customers would otherwise have no one to sort out their problems.

Q. How would you describe your time management skills? Are you good at time management?

Sample Ans.: I had a customer who wanted an emergency order dealt with immediately at the same time as my boss needed some financial data. There was no way I could have done both, so I asked a colleague to deal with the customer order while I put together the data that my boss needed.

Sample Ans.: I take on a very professional approach to time management. It's my habit to make schedules and timelines for work to complete my tasks before the deadline. I also make to-do lists and make sure to stick to my routines. These little things help me keep my days and weeks organized.

For time management, I believe there's nothing better than to-do lists and schedules. Once I have a list of tasks to do, I prioritize the tasks and then schedule them in my weekly/monthly schedule. I also follow a scheduling system for my meetings so that they never collide. This helps me to keep things well-planned and organized, both at work and at home.

Q. What makes you lose your temper?

Sample Ans.: I'm not the kind of person who ever gets angry at work. Anger just isn't productive and even in a crisis, it's more important to figure out what can be done to sort out the situation than to shout and scream and point the finger of blame at people.

Sample Ans.: I guess that sometimes I do let my frustration show. For example, when colleagues promise to do something and then let me down at the last moment, I have been known to have a few terse words with them.

Q. How do you cope with job stress?

Sample Ans.: No matter how bad the day I've had – perhaps it's due to a difficult case or just too much to do – when I get home, I get changed and go for a 20-minute jog. Whenever I do that, I can literally feel the tension leaving my body.

Q. Describe your ability to work under pressure.

Sample Ans.: I understand the nature of this position that I am applying for quite well, along with the pressure that comes with it. Being under pressure doesn't discourage me but motivates me more.

Q. How well can you handle stress and pressure?

Sample Ans.: While nobody can escape work pressure and stress, I believe that having an organized schedule can help a great deal. Also, prioritizing work is a must. I like to stay ahead of my timeline to deliver my tasks/projects on time. As for stress buster, I love to listen to calming music. It helps me keep my calm and continue with my work. For me, the most important thing is to keep a calm head. When you have a calm mind, it's much easier to figure out ways to handle stressful situations.

Sample Ans.: Being in the industry has helped me understand that pressure and stress are very much a part of the job. I am fully aware of the kind of pressure that comes with a particular position, and I'm up for it. I've never felt discouraged by pressure. Rather it motivates me to push myself and accomplish the task I'm set to do.

Q. Why are you leaving your current position?

Sample Ans.: I need to be challenged to develop my potential further. I'm interested in additional responsibility and new opportunities, which unfortunately are limited at my present company because of company size/limited product line/company restructuring or downsizing. The reputation and market focus of your company offers many opportunities for someone with my training and experience. It's the optimum kind of environment, I've been seeking.

Q. Which one job do you like most?

Sample Ans.: Only one? That's difficult to answer because I like everything about my chosen field. Yet, I like most the job of handling customer complaints which gives me a sense of pride that we're doing something important.

Q. What three areas of your job do you like least?

Sample Ans.: I can't think of any major dislikes. I guess my answers will have to come under the category of nuisances or annoyances. The biggest annoyance is other people who don't share the same sense of purpose or care about the company's goals—the kind of employees who are just putting in their time. It happens everywhere you work; but I can't help thinking that, if everyone would concentrate on the business at hand, we'd all accomplish even more.

Q. Describe the best supervisor you ever had.

Sample Ans.: My best supervisor was someone who expected a lot from me and taught me to expect a lot from myself. Then, she guided me through the training, knowledge, and experience that I needed to fulfill my potential and become a credit to the company. We discussed assignments, what was required, what I needed to do, and where I could find assistance, but; then she let me do my work my way. There was always a feeling of mutual respect and trust. I remember that as a time when we showed that teamwork could accomplish a great deal. It was a pleasure to go to work in the morning and leave at night with a sense of accomplishment. Knowing her helped me develop my leadership skills. Although it's been years since we worked together, her methods serve as a strong guide for my own leadership decisions.

Q. Describe the best job you ever had.

Sample Ans.: As you're aiming at the target job, know what that job requires and describe one very similar. If your description of your best job is the complete opposite of the target job, you'll be shooting off your toes. My best job was the position of Administrator, at GECO LTD. It offered me the opportunity to use all my initiative and skills to solve problems and get things done. At times the pace was fast, but things were never out of control. Beneath it all were organization, structure, and guidelines that helped employees make decisions and accomplish their jobs effectively. There were policies and procedures, and scope to use creativity in my work. All these characterized a great job for me.

Q. What references would your current/previous employer will give you?

Sample Ans.: If are sure that favourable feedback about you will be given, you may say that you are confident that all my references will be favourable and will confirm what we've discussed here today. If you suspect that any unavoidable reference might be negative, you may say although I'm proud of the work I did there, and always did my best, my supervisor and I never seemed to overcome some philosophical differences. It was just one of those things that happens occasionally even in the most successful careers. I made the best of it, cut my losses, and moved on. Even though people

Q. How would you compare the quality of your work to that of others in the same job?

Sample Ans.: The quality of my work has been consistently as good as or better than that of my coworkers. I've always met or exceeded expectations. I set my pace according to what is required by the job, and I always try to beat the clock and my record. If I just kept doing the average work, at an average pace, life would be boring. So, I don't wait for challenges.

Q. In what areas of your current job are you strongest?

Sample Ans.: Think about your strengths specific to the work you do and the target job and script your answer in the following lines, "my strengths are my ability to find the fastest, most efficient way to get the work done meeting the parameters. I get along with seniors, coworkers, and subordinates. [now add the specific area of your job in which you are strong]

Q. In what areas of your current job you are weakest?

Sample Ans.: As you have to sell yourself into a job, avoid revealing any major weaknesses. Just mention something benign that shows you're human before you take the pre-employment physical. For example, you may say," I don't have any major weaknesses that interfere with how I do my work. The only area where I occasionally fall behind is in completing my daily activity reports fast for which I stay late and get them done."

Q. What factors contribute most to your success in your current job?

Sample Ans.:   First, exposure and experience of handling multiple activities associated with the job. Added to this is the training I received in my previous jobs helped me go further and faster on this job. My jobs have increased in responsibility, with each level building on the last. Second, continuing education. I attended seminars and workshops and take courses, and I always have professional or management materials available to read. The third reason for my success, is good planning and productive use of time. When I run into roadblocks on the job, I figure out a way to eliminate them. If Plan A is temporarily on hold, I immediately swing into plans B, C, D, and so on. It's amazing how much nonproductive time can be turned into job improvement if you're just aware of how to do it.

Q. What do your supervisors think are your strengths?

Sample Ans.: From what they've told me informally and formally during performance reviews, they think I'm a productive and efficient employee and a good team player. I've had particularly high ratings in meeting objectives, completing assignments on time, and working well with coworkers to accomplish company objectives.

Q. What do your supervisors think are your weaknesses?

Sample   Ans.:   Although   my   evaluations   have   been overwhelmingly   favourable,   I   have   occasionally   received comments about needing improvement in the area of record keeping/filing/ expense accounting. It's not that I don't meet the requirements in those areas. It's just that sometimes I get so intent on achieving something major by a certain deadline that, occasionally, these routine functions are delayed while I'm immersed in a major project or problem.

Q. What is your current boss's title and what are his or her duties?

Sample Ans.: She is the Marketing Manager reporting to the Regional General Manager of Marketing. She is responsible for overseeing the work of the department, which consists of ten marketing executives and three office staff. The department is responsible for supporting a national marketing force of twenty-five employees, preparing their leads, and correspondence, processing orders, making sure salespeople follow up on all leads, and maintaining distributor relationships.

Q. Describe a typical day in your job.

Sample Ans.: I arrive early to review my things today which I prepared yesterday. I assign priorities to listed jobs. There are many interruptions throughout the day. The phone rings, and suddenly there's a major breakdown to immediately attend. It's unavoidable. I keep those objectives in mind and accomplish them one at a time between all the emergencies. I stay levelheaded. My good planning and time management skills help me stay on top of the work, so my coworkers and I enjoy meeting new challenges while we keep the department moving along.

Q. Would you recommend your current company for a job to others?

Sample Ans.: Certainly, depending on the kind of work they were seeking and their attributes. There is interesting work there for people who can produce. As I might have mentioned before, I am seeking another position because my growth there is limited by company size in my branch.

Q. Have you made any contributions to publications in your field?

Sample Ans.: (If published). Yes, I have. I've had articles published in the Quarterly Issue of (XYZ) magazine and the six-monthly issue of (ABC) Journal of DKG. I have copies of them right here in my briefcase that I'd be pleased to give you if you'd like.

Sample Ans.: (If not published). Not yet. I pursued study on writing articles. I am comfortable now. I have some ideas for articles and several outlines. I'm comfortable completing the articles and submitting them for publication.

Q. Have you ever walked out on a job?

Sample Ans.: In my last employment, when I felt a negative situation that I could not have managed, I carefully planned my exit, secured another position first, and gave my employer adequate notice to allow a smooth transition to my replacement.
Sample Ans.: Yes, I had to make a painful decision to leave one company even before I had secured a new job. In that job, I worked very hard, every day long hours, and did my best to turn the negative situation around without any cooperation. As long as I was in that job, I couldn't get away to interview for a new one. Finally, I gave my notice, leaving only when I had found and trained my replacement. I secured the ideal job within six weeks and performed my new assignment effectively and happily.

Q. Why do you want to leave your present job? Why are you looking for a job?

Sample Ans.: I feel like I've learned all that I possibly could in my present organization, and now, I'm looking for something different. I want to explore new avenues and am more than willing to take on challenging roles.

Sample Ans.: I feel like it's time to expand my horizons. I've been with my present organization for quite some time, and while I'm grateful for all that I've learned there, I want to go beyond my current role. And I feel that your company is the perfect place for me to challenge myself and push my limits.

Q. What is your work ethic?

Sample Ans.: I've always been organized and planned with my schedule. Even during my academic days, I was a very disciplined student. I like planning my schedule and following it diligently. My aim as a professional is always to deliver quality work within due time. I believe no job is menial and that all tasks should be given equal importance.

Sample Ans.: My work ethic lies in my diligence, commitment, and passion for my work. So far, in my professional life, I've worked dedicatedly to never miss a deadline without compromising my work quality. I believe that teamwork and collaboration go a long way into creating a healthy work environment.

Q. Can you explain the long gaps in your employment history?

Sample Ans.: In my first job, I realized that to foster my career, I needed more education and training. I left the job and went for regular college courses. My decision proved to be perfect. I learnt critical skills and time management. In this backdrop, I joined the same organization at a higher level. Another time, my job was not adding to my computer programming knowledge and my job was stable. So, I switched the job. However, my track record for the past years has been consistent and progressive, and my work has increased in responsibility. I have set my career goals and have developed a plan for achieving them which combined with my family responsibilities, makes me a very stable employee.

Q. Why have you had many jobs for short periods?

Sample Ans.: Yes, my career marked job changes after short periods. I accepted an entry-level job on the basis that I would be promoted within six months. After a year of working, I did not get a response to my reminding them of their assurance of promoting me. I realized I'd need to move out to move up. In another situation, my department was reorganized shortly after I was hired, and I was moved into an unrelated position that didn't fit my background and skills. I tried to make it work for six months, but it was obvious there was a mismatch. I did a good job, but I just wasn't happy. It wasn't my field. In every job, I've given my best effort and made it work. In recent years, my work record has been more stable. That's due to of the lessons I've learned. I'm more careful now to be sure, I'm going after something that will work out for my employer and myself.

Q. What is the highest accomplishment you can name from each of your previous jobs?

Sample Ans.: I devised a system for handling customer orders that reduced the average waiting time from six minutes to four minutes per customer. We were able to increase sales during rush periods by 30 percent. As a result, my system was adopted for use companywide. As a district manager for the same company, I instituted employee incentive programs for customer service.

Q. What do you consider the most significant accomplishment in your entire career?

Sample Ans.: At GECO, I worked for the first three years of my career so far. While working with them, my most significant accomplishment was my rising from the post of a Trainee to Junior Manager. It did not have shift duty. I joined night courses in Business Administration. I asked for more responsibility and opportunity for me. It so happened that I was associated with coordinating the company's annual Foundation Day event. My managing capability was noticed by higher management. I've since completed my Business Administration Degree and displayed my abilities at the job, I was uplifted to position from a Trainee to Junior Manager. This became the most significant accomplishment in my entire career as it became a turning point in my career that made all the other subsequent achievements possible

Q. Have you had a chance to upgrade your skills to the level currently required?

Sample Ans.: Yes, I have been upgrading my skills. I meet the requirements of this job. I'm comfortable with my ability to handle this position with only a very brief orientation into the company's specific procedures. From here, I hope to continue further improving and expanding my skills and abilities.

Q. In what areas have you received compliments from your superiors?

Sample Ans.: I have always had high marks in job effectiveness, initiative, and enthusiasm. I look at each assignment as an exciting challenge. My managers say I create spirited teamwork, less absenteeism, and higher output.

Q. Did your company increase its (sales/profits) this year?

Sample Ans.: Yes, sales were up 7 percent in the last quarter, and 10 percent over the last three quarters from the previous year. Net profit as a percentage of sales increased from 6 to 8 percent. We've had a very good year.

Q. Name five reasons for your success.

Sample Ans.: One, my high energy and effective skills lead to high work output. Two, I place a strong emphasis on improving the quality in products and services. Three, I continue to improve and polish my skills and abilities. Fourth, I try to look at old problems from new perspectives and to come up with a creative approach that leads to a workable solution. Finally, I take responsibility seriously and make it my priority to give an honest day's work for an honest day's pay—every day.

Q. How would you know you were successful on this job?

Sample Ans.: Being successful means goals that are set are being met. Being successful also means standards are not only reached but also exceeded wherever possible.

Q. Describe your management style.

Sample Ans.: Basically, my management style comes with promptness and flexibility. To make sure goals are achieved, I religiously study and make plans down to the smallest detail. While I do implement a strict sense of being time-bound, I also add reasonable allowances and make room for contingencies.

Q. What will you do if you don't get this position?

Sample Ans.: I have high hopes that I will be hired. In case it turns the other way around, I would have to move on and search for another job.

Chapter 7
Goals & Stability

Q. Assuming, we hire you, how long would you be with us? How long will you stay with the company?

Sample Ans.1
As long as I feel like I'm contributing to the growth of your company while also undergoing personal growth, I will be loyal to the organization. I need job satisfaction and scope for professional development. So, if I continue to learn new things and scale up the promotional ladder, I will never feel the need to jump ships.
Sample Ans.2
I will happily continue to work with your company as long as there's mutual growth. While I'll contribute actively to promote the organization's growth, I will also expect to get ample opportunities to grow both professionally and financially.
Sample Ans.3
I look forward to staying as long as I'm productive. I shall continue to learn and develop my capabilities. I believe that, as long as I perform well on the job and make contributions, I'll be considered a valuable employee. And as long as I'm making a contribution that is valued, I'll have no reason to leave. However, if for any reason I don't meet the company's expectations, I don't expect to remain on the company's payroll
Sample Ans.4
If I enjoy working here and I feel like I have a bright future ahead of me, I'll be a dedicated and loyal employee of your organization. I'm looking forward to a healthy work environment where I can upskill and grow personally and professionally. As long as I find these aspects here, I'll never think about changing my job.

Q. What holds more importance for you: work or money?

Sample Ans.1
For me, work is a priority. I feel like if I'm satisfied with what I do and if I'm good at it, money will follow. My goal is to keep learning and upskilling. As my professional skills continue to grow, my professional worth will naturally increase.
Sample Ans.2
Being of a practical mindset, money has always been an important factor in my life. However, I firmly believe that if my work fails to satisfy me at the

end of the day, I won't be able to enjoy the money I earn. So, work will always be my foremost priority, and if I can prove my mettle in the workplace, I will be adequately rewarded.

Q. Where do you see yourself five years from now?

Sample Ans.1
In this position, I plan to add skills and experience. Honestly, I would like to move into a management role in technical support within five years. Once I've gained sufficient experience, I'd love to move on to a management position. What I like about this company is how they actively develop employees. I feel like I can consistently improve here and move into bigger roles for your organization.
Sample Ans.2
At least five years from now, I see myself working for this company. My job will have increased by at least one, probably two levels in responsibility and scope. I'll have made a significant contribution to the department and will be working on new ways to ladder into general/higher management

Q. Where would you see yourself in the next 10 years?

Sample Ans.: I would like to see myself in a so-and-so position managing a so-and-so team with the company's stats becoming so-and-so.

Q. Do you have any idea to study further or work only?

Sample Ans.: I want to get involved in the company's growth and progress first, if the company requires higher qualifications for certain promotions or posts, then only may opt for higher education for the company's benefit.

Q. Have you interviewed anywhere else?

Sample Ans.1: Yes, I'm actively looking for other great roles like this.
Sample Ans.2: I'm moving quickly with other companies with good roles and competitive offers.

Q. Can you tell us about your goals?

Sample Ans.: Tips: If you have applied to a technical role and your goal is to be in the management sector, tell them you would take this as a challenge to become a manager in the next 10 years and not about your career quit, to join the management degree.

Q. What are your long-term career objectives?

Sample Ans.: Give specific details about the field or profession first and then about the level you hope to attain within it. Then you may say, "I have given my career and opportunities a great deal of thought, and from that process, I've developed a plan for achieving my long-term objective. This position is an important step in that long-term plan.

Q. How important to you is the opportunity to reach the top?

Sample Ans.: I complete my work to the best of my ability and trust that, if I prove myself to be an asset to my employer, I'll be rewarded. So, although the opportunity to reach the top is important to me, I know that opportunity presents itself only to those who earn it.

Q. Why do you want this job?

Sample Ans.: Because of the challenge and the opportunities associated with this job? My career goal is to make a mark in the field (XYZ), and this job would allow me to develop my potential further while actively participating in that kind of work. This is exactly the kind of progressive technically oriented (use an adjective appropriate to the company and type of work) atmosphere I've been looking for.

Q. How long will you stay with the company?

Sample Ans.: I look forward to staying as long as I'm productive. I shall continue to learn and develop my capabilities. I believe that, as long as I perform well on the job and make contributions, I'll be considered a valuable employee. And as long as I'm making a contribution that is valued, I'll have no reason to leave. However, if for any reason I don't meet the company's expectations, I don't expect to remain on the company's payroll.

Q. What do you picture yourself doing(five/ten) years from now?
Sample Ans.: In this position, I plan to add skills and experience. Honestly, I would like to move into a management role in technical support within five years. Once I've gained sufficient experience, I'd love

to move on to a management position. What I like about this company is how they actively develop employees. I feel like I can consistently improve here and move into bigger roles for your organization."

Sample Ans.: At least five years from now, I see myself working for this company. My job will have increased by at least one, probably two levels in responsibility and scope. I'll have made a significant contribution to the department and will be working on new ways to ladder into general/higher management.

Q. Where would you see yourself in the next 10 years?

Sample Ans.: I would like to see myself in so-and-so position managing so-and-so team with company's stats becoming so-and-so

Q. What are your long-term career objectives?

Sample Ans.: Give specific details about the field or profession first and then about the level you hope to attain within it. Then you may say, "I have given my career and opportunities a great deal of thought, and from that process, I've developed a plan for achieving my long-term objective. This position is an important step in that long-term plan."

Q. Would you consider a switch in careers at this point in your life?

Sample Ans.: Possibly; I'm very happy with my chosen field and have done well in it, however, I believe in being flexible and open to new opportunities. If you have a position in mind for me in the company that is different from the work I've been doing, I'd like to explore it. I'm always interested in seeing how my background and skills can contribute to my success at a particular job There are things I can do even better as I progress upward.

Q. Would you be willing to relocate in the future?

Sample Ans.: Definitely, yes. When I have moved or relocated in the past, new worlds of opportunity opened for me. Any major change, while always containing some risk, is a chance to grow, learn, and advance. All I need is a few days' notice, and I'll be ready.

Q. Do you want to be president of this company?

Sample Ans.: Yes, I don't know too many capable, ambitious people who don't aspire to the highest management level within their companies. I aspire but I perspire, too. It gets better results. I also realize that there are many other steps along the way through which I can learn, contribute, and be rewarded for my work. I want to do the best job I can, moving on to the next challenge when I'm ready. If I continue to do that, I'll automatically rise to the top.

Q. Would you like to have your (current/previous) boss's job?

Sample Ans.: Yes. I have been assisting my boss in his jobs. I learned a lot and experienced even micro details of those jobs. I love my boss's job. In that sense, I guess you could say I'm interested in my boss's job. For companies to grow and improve, the people who work there must grow and improve. Promotion and advancement within the ranks are signs that a company provides opportunities and recognizes the potential of its employees.

Q. When do you expect a promotion?
Sample Ans.: Would like my career to continue progressing as well as it has in the past. But I'm a realist. I know promotions aren't given; they're earned. When I've mastered my present position, have improved it with my ideas, have prepared myself to take on new responsibilities, and have trained someone to take over my job, I'll be ready for a promotion.

Chapter 8

Joining & Leaving

Q. Why are you leaving your company?

Sample Ans.: I want to be a key player on a driven, talented team. I'm excited to grow and develop my skills and tackle new opportunities.

Q. Where else are you interviewing?

Sample Ans.: I've been interviewing at the three top firms. But I would much rather work for your organisation, because I feel that I will probably have a chance to learn more here, much faster, than at a larger firm. I learnt that your company gives first-year associates a great deal of responsibility when it comes to servicing clients.

Q. You have changed careers before. Why should I let you experiment on my magazine firm?

Sample Ans.: Most people change their careers eight times during their lives. I've only changed careers three times, I think I'm behind the eight ball, at least statistically. *[Be sure to crack a smile, so that your interviewer will also.]* I believe that I've gained a lot of diverse skills from moving around. These skills help me solve problems creatively. My first job as a.......... gave me the patience to explain the same set of facts, in different ways, to people who might have resisted earlier. My second job, working for an accountant, gave me a facility with spreadsheets and numbers. My third job, working in the circulation department of a magazine, helped me understand how to translate complicated numbers to ad agencies with limited amounts of money. All in all, I feel that my varied background makes me the ideal candidate for ad Sales Director at your magazine. By working in circulation, I've picked up a lot about marketing already. And the fact that I've switched careers a couple of times proves that I'm a very quick learner.

Q. I can see from your resume that you have moved around and changed jobs a lot. Do you get bored in a job quickly and find yourself wanting to move on?

Sample Ans.: Not at all. I embrace new challenges, certainly, but the reason that I job-hopped was to bring my salary up to a living wage. I needed to move jobs a bit just to pay my rent! But now that I'm on track financially, I'm looking for a position where I can grow on the job. I'm very excited about the prospect of working for your company because I know several people here who worked hard and were recognized for their achievements.

Q. You live an hour and a half away from the office. Most nights, we stick around until 9 p.m. How will you ever be able to survive working here?

Sample Ans.: For me, my commute home is my "quiet time" to relax, de-stress and unwind. I love taking the train. No one disturbs me, and the ride up to ….., even late at night, is gorgeous. At the end of the day, if I still have work on my desk, I'll just take it with me and finish it on the train. And if I don't, I'll use the time to catch up on a couple of newspapers, listen to a favorite music, and think about tomorrow's challenges.

Q. Do you see yourself staying and growing at our company, or leaving in two years to go to business school?

Sample Ans.: I might go to law or business school in a few years, but I'm 99 per cent certain that I'll choose one where I can go at night. So, there will be no break in my stay at your company. I've been interviewing at several of the smaller companies, but I would much rather start at a big firm like yours because I know that doing so will expose me to several disciplines. If you hire me, I intend to stay here for many years to come.

Q. From your resume, I notice that you interned for a small investment banking company. Did you pursue a full-time job offer with them? What happened?

Sample Ans.: Yes, I did very well at my internship, and I had originally assumed that I would come on staff once I graduated from college. However, TRANSMINT dropped their planning of new hires. They will not be hiring any of the interns they had last summer. I loved working at TRANSMINT, and I brought some references with me today to show you that my job performance there was stellar. Still, in some ways, I consider this new turn of events to be a lucky break for me, believe it or not. I've always had dreams of joining a more prestigious firm like yours. Your company's training program is the best in the business, and I know that if I come and work for you, I'll be on the correct track for my career ambitions.

Q. If we offer you a position and you accept it; how soon thereafter can you begin to work?

Sample Ans.: After giving my current employer two weeks' notice. I have the enthusiasm and energy to get started. Some people like to take a vacation between jobs, but a vacation should be earned. I might have earned a vacation on my last job, but I intend to prove myself here at the earliest opportunity.

Q. Why are you interested in this job?

Sample Ans.: Because it offers everything I've been looking for, the roles, the opportunity to learn, the overall environment and growth prospects. It fits perfectly with my career plans.

Q. Why would you be happy doing this type of work?

Sample Ans.: Because it's the kind of work I've always enjoyed doing. All the tests I took early in my career said I was best suited for this kind of work. I agreed and made my career plans accordingly. We like what we do best, and we do best what we like most!

Q. Do you feel confident in your ability to handle this position?

Sample Ans.:   Surely! I'm familiar with the basic job requirements. It should take me only a short time to become familiar with this company's procedures and methods. The sooner I learn what is expected of me, the sooner I can excel in the job. I don't like to waste time when there's a job to do. It undoubtedly will require extra time and effort on my part in the beginning, but I'm more than willing to devote that time and effort because it enables me to do the job right the first time and every time.

Q. Do you feel you are ready for a more responsible position? Tell me why you think so.

Sample Ans.: Yes, definitely. When you cease to be challenged, you stop growing. I've gone as far as I can go in my present job. My manager is very pleased with my work, but this post adds additional responsibility in the foreseeable future. I know I am capable of greater achievements, which is why I'm interviewing for this position. There's a challenge offered here that I'm ready to meet.

Q. Is there one particular trait or skill you possess that should lead us to consider you above other candidates?

Sample Ans.: (Tips: Think of your particular abilities and how they apply to the target job. Then tell and sell. Are you fast at the keyboard or a programmer? If the job involves customer service or is otherwise people-oriented, do you have the ability to make others respond favourably? Be sure to mention what you think is the most prominent of your own unique and proven skills. Then close with the addition that, "I have the drive to take on this job and to do it well. I think I'll excel at it.)

Q. May we contact your present employer?

Sample Ans.: *(If, you have officially informed your employer that you are interviewing.)*
Yes, my employer knows I am interviewing and understands the reason. My boss even told me recently, "That's the price you sometimes pay for hiring and training the best people." We've had a good working relationship for the past ever since I joined there. But now I've reached the highest level possible there, and I've trained people to assume my duties. My boss regrets not being able to offer me more at this time. We will be parting on good terms. All of what I've told you will be confirmed when you call. But please let me know first so I can let the boss down gently."

Sample Ans.: *(If, you have officially not informed your employer that you are interviewing, while answering this question don't giggle and say that)*
I haven't told my employer. So please let me know before you contact anyone there. Once there's a firm offer on the table, or you've narrowed the field to only a few candidates, the information I've given you can be verified. My boss deserves the courtesy of hearing I'm leaving. She'll be upset, but I'll assure her that everything will be done to most efficient transfer of my duties. You'll probably get more than a reference and testimonial.

Q. Are you willing to start as a trainee?

Sample Ans.: *(In case, you are willing to start as a trainee.)*
Yes, definitely. As a trainee, I believe in getting a good foundation in the basics before progressing which I'm sure will contribute to my rapid progress. If I learn at my usual pace, I expect to be assuming greater responsibility when it becomes available".

Sample Ans.: *(If you do not want to begin as a trainee.)*
I have sufficient experience in this area, it will not take time for me to learn the specific methods and procedures this company uses. As such, I'd be wasting your management's time as a trainee, and that wouldn't be in the company's best interests.

Q. Why do you want to enter this field?

Sample Ans.:   I want to be where things are developing, changing, and growing. From the research I've done, there appears to be tremendous opportunity in this field. I want to spend my career in an industry and a company where the horizon is always expanding, and there is always new territory to cover. I'll learn something new or solve a problem I've never faced before—one that will require all my talent.

Q. What do you think about how we run our operation?

Sample Ans.:   Whatever, I've researched and heard, I see a vibrant, responsive organization. A good measure of a company is in the enthusiasm of its employees, and the people here sure demonstrate that.

Q. Do you think your lack of *a degree* will affect your ability to perform the job?

274. Sample Ans.:   No, I don't think it will have an adverse effect. I don't have the traditional academic letters after my name, but, my experience and learning is enough to compensate related academic degree. Education is an ongoing process throughout life. I find myself learning all the time. When it comes to my job, I'm very practical. If something will make me better at what I do, I want to learn all I can about it. I'm confident I have the knowledge and skill to get the job done and even to find new ways of doing it more efficiently and effectively.

Q. Do you think your lack of *experience* will affect your ability to perform the job?

Sample Ans.:   I might not have years of experience in this profession, but I know necessary to make an impressive start and have the willingness to learn and improve. I have the skills required by this position. I learn quickly and will work hard to prove myself. Training is much easier than un-training. I think you'll be impressed by how quickly I learn and how much I accomplish in this position.

Q. Aren't you overqualified for this job?

276.Sample Ans.: It's the job and role that matters for an incumbent. With my qualifications, I can do the job right away. The company will benefit from my additional experience, and I'll be able to do more with the position. I'll continue to be challenged and I will be acquiring additional job experience. I'd welcome the opportunity to use what I know to improve things here. So, while I might be starting at a slightly lower level of responsibility, this company is growing and going places. I see a lot of opportunities here.

Chapter 9

Qualification Questions

Q. Why did you attend that particular college?

Sample Ans.: I chose XYZ because of its competitive atmosphere and good reputation. Although I could have attended other colleges, this one emphasized practical, job-related courses and student participation in activities related to their specific career plans. Many of my friends found themselves going to colleges their parents had chosen, but I set my own educational and career goals. XYZ might have been a little more expensive than some of the other colleges, but this forced me to work harder because I helped pay my way. I'm pleased with my decision. I relied on my instincts, and they paid off. Now I'm extremely optimistic about my future because my college education also taught me self-reliance, time management, and the value of hard work.

Q. Did your family have any influence on your choice of college?

Sample Ans.: My family had several suggestions to make, but they realized I was pretty sure of myself and knew what I wanted. They stood back and let me decide. They agreed with my decision when I shared the results of my research with them.

Q. What was your major in college?
Sample Ans.: I majored in ---- with a minor in ----.

Q. What made you choose____________ as your major?

Sample Ans.1
(The answer for an interviewee who majored in a subject or area that directly applies to their careers.)
I always knew that .... (IT or ICT, BCA, MCA) was where I had the most potential, and I've remained with it because I turned out to be right. Not everyone is as fortunate as I have

been. It's very difficult at 18 to predict and plan for the future; but, even then, I knew what I wanted to do. I'm glad I set my goals at a young age. It has worked out well for me."

Sample Ans.2
(The response for those who majored in one thing and are doing another.)
When I was 18, nothing in the world seemed so important as _ (History/Philosophy/English literature), and I studied for the sake of learning. Later, I realized I needed further education in subjects that would help me in my career.

Q. Do you feel you made the right choice?

Sample Ans.1
(The *answer for an interviewee who majored in a subject or area that directly applies to their careers.)*
Absolutely, and my career success bears me out. I am very happy with the path my life and work have followed.

Sample Ans.2
(The response for those who majored in one thing and are doing another.)
I'm glad I started in one area and switched to another. It has enhanced my ability to be creative and flexible because I have learned different approaches to performing the work successfully.

Q. How have your education and training prepared you for the job?

Sample Ans.: My education gave me the tools to succeed, and my training taught me how to do the job properly. Before I knew what, my job entailed, I only thought I would perform it well. The training allowed me to apply my education. By having the chance to do the work expected of me in advance, I gained the confidence to meet future challenges and the experience to do so successfully. The real challenge starts where the education and training end. Studying diligently and practising constantly really paid off. Now I am confident in my work and have earned the respect of my co-workers.

Q. What specialized training have you received to improve your job skills?
(Tips: From the three choices given, choose one answer that most closely applies to your situation.)

Sample Ans.1
After beginning my career, I saw that my ___ (high school diploma/vocational education/undergraduate degree) wasn't enough. I needed knowledge of a higher and more specific level, so I went back to school to get a __ (bachelor/master) of ______, which I (will complete/complete) in ____. By integrating my studies with actual job experience, I found I could leverage the value I received through my education. I estimate I learned about 10 times as much that specifically applies to this field during my ______ (graduate) work.

Sample Ans.2
I took every opportunity that arose to attend classes, seminars, and workshops in this area. Even when my employer wasn't sponsoring the education, I used my own money and personal time to learn what I needed to know. It paid off. (If you can, mention two or three well-known and reputable seminars, especially those linked to schools prominent in the field—such as Wharton, Stanford, or AMA-sponsored seminars for management candidates.)

Sample Ans.3
I know education is important. When we stop learning, we stop growing and achieving. Since I began my career _____ years ago, I have been so thoroughly occupied with the demands of work that my ongoing education has been through on-the-job learning, company-sponsored training, and similar activities. I read everything I can find that applies to my profession, subscribe to its trade journals, and keep myself current on new developments.

Q. Why didn't you continue your formal education?

Sample Ans.: Two reasons. The first was my impatience to earn rather than learn. The second reason was that I enjoyed being productive. As I mentioned, I worked part-time to pay my college expenses, and I was fortunate to be employed by some excellent companies. My employers always seemed to want more of my time and talents, and in many cases, I was working at levels beyond what I was studying in my classes. Finally, I left school in my __ year and devoted myself full-time to my career. I've never regretted that decision because I have continued to learn and grow with my work.

Q. How did you do in school?
(Tips: You may choose either of the following replies as it fits in your case.)

Sample Ans.1 Dean's list throughout, with a ________ grade point average.

Sample Ans.2
Above average—mostly Bs and some Cs. I worked and was involved in many extracurricular activities while maintaining a low B/high C average.

Sample Ans.3
My grades were average, but I spent a great deal of time achieving in other areas, such as part-time employment and extracurricular activities like __ (mention activities and affiliations related to target job). I always did my work thoroughly. As with most other people, if I could do it again, my grades probably would be much higher. I'd not only work harder, but I've learned a lot since then!

Q. How did you finance your education?

Sample Ans.: I worked part-time to pay expenses and (if applicable) had a financial aid package that included scholarships and student loans.

Q. Are you currently taking, or do you plan to take, any evening courses?

Sample Ans.: I am presently studying ZYZ__ at ___, which I find very valuable to my ongoing job performance and general knowledge. With the demands of keeping up with my job, I haven't signed up for anything this semester; but as soon as I've made a decision and settled into my new position, I'm sure I will be looking for courses in furtherance of my general and professional knowledge.

Q. Do you subscribe to trade or professional journals? Which ones?
Tips: If you don't subscribe now, get your hands on back issues and mail in your subscription orders before you begin interviewing. It makes career sense to be conversant about new developments in your profession, no matter what your current job level.
Sample Ans.: Yes, I subscribe to and read ________. *(Mention the most influential journals in your field.)* If you've ever contributed an article that was published, mention that as well.

Q. In the past year, have you attended any professional seminars or conferences at your own expense?
Tips: You may choose either of these responses as it suits you:

Sample Ans.1
Yes, I attended ___ in___ (month & year) and (if applicable, continue listing). My employer paid my registration fees.

Sample Ans.2
No, not in the past year, but at other times in the past I've attended seminars and workshops on _ and __ given by various organizations in the field. Because there are so many seminars available, it's important to be careful in making a selection. Otherwise, there would be no time left to apply what is learned. Because I'm selective, I always get something out of every educational program I attend. If a program is offered that would help me improve my knowledge or ability in my work, I'd attend on my own time and at my own expense.

Q. What are your educational goals for the future?

Sample Ans.: My goal is to do everything possible to keep learning and improving. Things change so rapidly that we cannot rely on what we learned 10, 5, or even 2 years ago. Some of my education will be informal reading, research, and simply paying attention to what is going on. You can learn a lot just by listening to the right people and watching them. Also, however, I am planning to take courses in XYZ course at ____________ (name of school) which will foster my professional career besides adding to my knowledge base.

Q. Did your grade point average reflect your work ability?
Sample Ans.: My grades were above average to excellent, and I think my work record has been the same. There is a different method of evaluation in school, of course, and I've worked harder on the job than I did in school. At work, it's results that count, and I've always been able to achieve results. It's not just what you know, but what you do with what you know. This has always been my formula for career success.

Q. Name three things you learned in school that could be used on this job.

Sample Ans.: What school taught me that has worked throughout my career was how to solve problems, how to apply myself, and, finally, how to set a goal and achieve it.

Q. What was your favourite subject in college?
Tips: Think of a subject that will mean something to a prospective employer. Invariably, this will be something job-related or business-oriented.)
Sample Ans.: The turning point for me was when I took a course in ___________. It opened my eyes to the possibilities in this business, and I found I had the potential to be successful at it.

Q. Did your college grades differ after military service?

Sample Ans.1: If no: then the answer is simply "No."

302.Sample Ans.2 *(If yes)*:
Yes, the military changes most people, because it demands self-discipline and self-reliance. I was a good student before the military but when I returned to school after I was discharged, there was a definite improvement in my grades. No excuses, only excellence. I wouldn't settle for less. I was there to learn.

Q. Have you ever been tutored? In what subjects?

Sample Ans.1 *(If no):*
No, I never had any particular difficulty in school.

Sample Ans.2 *(If yes):*
When I was in _________ (elementary/ junior high/high school), I needed tutoring for a brief period in _________ (English/math). It was beneficial to have one-on-one extra help like that. It helped me overcome a temporary obstacle and gave me an even stronger foundation in those skills.

Q. Why didn't you do better in school?

Sample Ans.: I guess I was just involved with other activities and growing up. I always got along with my teachers and classmates, and I even won awards for _______ (perfect attendance/science projects/debate club). The importance of grades did not have an impact on me then. Today I realize the value of formal academic achievement, and my career marks have always been well above average.

Chapter 10

Interrogation Questions

Q. How interested are you in sports?

Sample Ans.: I like playing them more than watching them.

Q. What are your leisure-time activities?
(Tips: Keep a script ready for this question. If this company appears to be activity-oriented, and you play racquetball but also collect stamps, emphasize racquetball.)

Sample Ans.: My dedication to my career takes up most of my time, however, I make it a point to spend time with my family every day. I'm involved in my kids' sports and help them with their homework. After that, I settle down and catch up on my work-related reading—journals and other trade publications. Weekends are spent in family activities, gardening, social events, and community affairs.

Q. What were your extracurricular activities in school?
(Tips: If the target job requires leadership skills.)

Sample Ans.1
I was captain of the debating team and vice president of the senior class.
Sample Ans.2
My extracurricular activities in high school and college centred around sports—mainly football and track.

Q. What newspaper do you read? What section do you turn to first?
(Tips: Keep script ready, given employer and target job. In this question, the second part of the question is the most important.)

Sample Ans.: I read the Wall Street Journal because it gives me a quick synopsis of international news and allows me to focus on economic trends that are important in my work. On weekend days, I read our local weekend paper to catch up on community affairs, local business activity, and commentary.

Q. What is your favourite television program?
(Tips: Try to chart a middle course.)

Sample Ans.: There isn't much time in my life for watching television, other than the evening news. Occasionally, I see if something is interesting to watch. I like business-oriented specials and news features the best.

Q. Can you name the Senators?

Sample Ans.: Of course! The senior senator is …XYZ… a (Party/Republican/Democrat).

Q. Have you ever been the head of a committee?

Sample Ans.: Yes, several times. Most recently, I chaired the annual fund-raising event for XYZ, a local service club. I've headed up several different committees for that organization in past years.

Q. Do you consider yourself a social drinker?

Tips: A moderate answer is your best bet here.
Sample Ans.: I enjoy an occasional glass of wine with a formal dinner. But I can take or leave alcohol in social situations. At business functions where clients are present, if I drink at all, it will be just one drink so I will be sure to stay alert and represent the company to the best of my ability.

Q. Does your social life include associates and co-workers?

Sample Ans.: I prefer to strike a good balance between my personal and professional activities. But I am sensitive to the needs of others. We're being paid to do a job, there's not much time for socializing when we're doing it.

Q. What kind of jobs did you have as a child?

Sample Ans.: My parents encouraged responsibility from an early age. I was assigned household chores from the age of ___ and began helping with the family business at the age of ______.

Q. The person you would be reporting to in this position is younger than you. Do you see that as problematic?

Sample Ans.:   Absolutely; not. I regard people from their achievements and capabilities, not on their age irrespective of race, gender, or ethnic origin.

Q. Describe what for you is an ideal workday.

Sample Ans.:   I set out tasks to-do-today, and prefer to accomplish those tasks with as little distraction. But; I'm not rigid and so am not waylaid by the inevitable interruptions or surprises. That way, when called on, I turn on my attention fully to a more pressing concern.

Q. What about your current job dissatisfies you and has compelled you to seek employment with us?

Sample Ans.: There is nothing wrong with my current employer and present job to make a new opportunity look right for me. I think of myself as a mover and a shaker, even if the only thing I am moving and shaking is me. My reason for applying for this job has all to do with my desire to continue to challenge myself and grow professionally.

Q. This job entails a lot of overtime. Can your relationships stand the strain?

Sample Ans.: I am fortunate that I have the full support of my family. I've always been upfront with them about what it will take to meet those goals. The time we spend together is quality time. Sometimes when there's less of a thing, it's better appreciated.

Q. What characteristics of a work environment do you find counterproductive?

Sample Ans.:   An environment that is too structured, too hierarchical, and tends to be rigid.

Q. What would you say if I were to tell you that, during this interview, you had failed to convince me you are right for this job?

Sample Ans.:   Failure of this sort is never pleasant, so my immediate response would be to express my disappointment. But I would try to learn something from it. I'd ask you, first, to clarify which questions I had failed to answer to your satisfaction. Next, I'd ask you to allow me to expand that answer. I would also ask you whether my style of communicating was faulty in any way.

Q. If you are hired, what do you plan to do in the first week (month) on the job?

Sample Ans.:   I would prefer to utilize a couple of weeks in a new job familiarizing myself with staff, company policies, and procedures, as well as my predecessor's actions and decisions. I would also like to focus on ………....are of job. However; I will enter into a crisis and will be acting immediately and decisively.

Q. What would you do if you were a victim of, or witness to, sexual harassment on the job, but you were afraid that reporting it or seeking to address it would be regarded by some of your colleagues as rocking the boat or not being a team player?

Sample Ans.:   Being a team player means that everyone on the team counts. The best way to proceed in such situations is to act quickly but judiciously according to company policy.

Q. Tell me quickly three words that describe your best character traits, and then three that describe your worst.

Sample Ans.:   Best: conscientious, trustworthy, self-sufficient. Worst: intense, competitive, perfectionist.

Q. Of the three worst weaknesses you listed, which causes you the most trouble?

Sample Ans.: I wish to complete the job in hand with perfection as meticulously as possible. But, on occasion, I've reluctantly let it go halfway. I'm told, "It's good enough and it's time to move on." I have no trouble hearing this, however; I dig in my heels as I feel a failing in a project that will ultimately forestall its success.

Q. According to your resume, you have been with XYZ Company for seven years. This company is known to have a well-established. Do you think you will have trouble adapting to the tenor of our organization, which is much smaller and younger and has a culture still in flux and not well-defined?

Sample Ans.: In fact, I welcome the opportunity to stretch myself in this way. Nothing enables a professional to grow so much as to make a move from a more bureaucratic structure to one with an entrepreneurial flavour, where it is often possible to be more creative and make more innovative choices.

Q. I noticed you also held the same position in that company for several of those years. Why?

Sample Ans.:   Though my title remained the same, my responsibilities did not, nor did my salary. My skills continued to develop and I went on being motivated by new and challenging goals. My position at that company was fulfilling to me professionally and stimulating intellectually, for as long as I held it.

Q. This job involves enough travel, within the country and abroad demanding a tremendous physical and mental toll. At this stage in your career, are you prepared to meet this demand?

Sample Ans.: I know that to do a job to the best of my ability, I have to make self-care a top priority. I exercise regularly, eat right, and pay attention to what my body tells me. Not only am I prepared, I feel more confident in my ability to do so now than ever before. At the beginning of my career, I was somewhat casual about taking care of myself. Today, I know that to do a job to the best of my ability, I have to make self-care a top priority. To that end, I exercise regularly, eat right, and pay attention to what my body tells me—which is as important a form of communication as any.

Q. What single trait of a supervisor, current or past, has caused a problem for you?

Sample Ans.: The trait of micromanager or very close supervision. He/she has to be involved in every decision I make, and every step, I take. I'm a highly skilled professional, and know for what I was hired. I kept myself concerned with my performance and paid attention to my functions without assigning blame or issuing a complaint against that person.

Q. If you are hired, what do you plan to do in the first week (month) on the job?

Sample Ans.: Barring stepping into a crisis that requires me to act immediately and decisively, I always think it's wise to spend the first couple of weeks in a new job familiarizing myself with staff, company policies, and procedures, as well as my predecessor's actions and decisions.

Q. What reassurance do we have that this will not be a temporary diversion for you until something more appropriate comes along?

Sample Ans.: My roles in my previous jobs, as mentioned in my resume, on the face of them, might not seem directly related to those identified for this position. However; I can assure you that my experience and skills are not only fully adaptable to this job, but they uniquely position me to bring a fresh approach to meeting the requirements included in this job description. If you wish, I'd like to detail how my past experience qualifies me for this job. Finally, because I believe this position to be entirely appropriate, I do not regard it to be temporary in any way.

Q. Describe a situation when you lost it on the job when you failed to remain objective or to behave professionally.

Sample Ans.: I can honestly say I've never totally lost control in front of staff or colleagues. That's not to say I haven't felt like it or haven't honestly expressed my unhappiness or disappointment to staff on occasion; but whenever I have felt on the verge of saying or doing something unacceptable in a business situation, I step away literally, take a break, go for a walk, get a cup of coffee.

Q. What would you do if you were a victim of, or witness to, sexual harassment on the job, but you were afraid that reporting it or seeking to address it would be regarded by some of your colleagues as rocking the boat or not being a team player?

Sample Ans.: Being a team player means that everyone on the team counts including someone being treated in an unprofessional manner or someone being accused unjustly. The best way to proceed in such situations is to act quickly but judiciously, and always according to company policy.

Q. This is a three-part question: First, what is the harshest criticism ever levelled at you by a supervisor, current or past? Second, was it warranted? Third, how did you handle it?

Sample Ans.: Once, during a high-pressure brainstorming staff meeting at which almost everyone in the division was present, I put up a suggestion that was a viable alternative to the idea my boss was promoting. Later, he called me into his office and said that what I had done was undermining his authority and insubordination. I realized why he so felt as several other staff were present in the meeting. I confess I was stunned. Nevertheless, I was confident he had misinterpreted my intent, so I explained calmly that my objective had been only to ensure that we had an alternative option in hand to resolve the issue and not to reject his suggestion. Then I also assured him that I would, in the future, be more careful about how and when I speak out, keeping in mind how it might be seen by others.

Q. According to your resume, you have been with XYZ Corporation for 15 years. This company is known to have a well-established—some might even say entrenched—culture. Do you think you will have trouble adapting to the tenor of our organization, which is much smaller and younger at only five years in existence and has a culture still in flux and not always well-defined?

Sample Ans.: The newer company has a more formal structure. I am known among my colleagues and friends as someone who adapts smoothly and quickly to new situations and environments. I welcome the opportunity to stretch myself in this way. Nothing enables a professional to grow so much as making a move from a more bureaucratic structure to one with an entrepreneurial set-up where it is often possible to be more creative and make more innovative choices.

Q. I noticed you also held the same position in that company for several of those years. Why?

Sample Ans.: Though my title remained the same, my responsibilities did not, nor did my salary. As a result, my skills continued to develop and I went on being motivated by new and challenging goals. My position at XYZ Company was fulfilling to me professionally and stimulating to me intellectually, for as long as I held it.

Q. What single trait of a supervisor, current or past, has caused a problem for you?

Sample Ans.: I have found it difficult to flourish under a micromanager, someone who has to be involved in every decision I make, and every step I take. I'm a highly skilled professional and assume that's why I was hired, and so expect to be trusted to do my job. When I faced this situation, I dealt with it upfront. I set up a meeting with my boss and asked him/her, pointedly but respectfully, whether there was anything about my performance prompting him/her to monitor my work in this close fashion. This turned out to be exactly the right thing to do: By demonstrating that I was concerned about my performance, I was able to direct attention to the problem without assigning blame or issuing a complaint.

Q. Describe a situation when you lost it on the job—when you failed to remain objective or to behave professionally.

Sample Ans.: I can honestly say I've never totally lost control in front of staff or colleagues. That's not to say I haven't felt like it. or haven't honestly expressed my unhappiness or disappointment to staff on occasion; but whenever I have felt on the verge of saying or doing something unacceptable in a business situation, I step away—literally—take a break, go for a walk, get a cup of coffee. To drive home your point, it's a good idea to give a specific example and conclude if that if you had stayed angry, you and your company would have missed an opportunity to gain.

Chapter 11

Personal Life Management Questions

(Tips: These questions relate to how you arrange your personal life. Personal decisions provide clues to your attitude and behaviour which impacts performance on the job. Answer such questions in such a way that will show responsible, mature attitudes and actions now, even if there are some hazy spots in your past.

In answering questions about your parent's occupation, avoid saying anything negative, like "My father was just a janitor" or "My mother didn't work." Show pride in your background and heritage, even if you have come to regard it as very humble. Be careful about overstating, too. Avoid an answer like "My father is the leading brain surgeon in the state and my mother is a retired Superior Court judge.)

Q. What are your parents' occupations?

Sample Ans.1
My father was a custodial supervisor, and my mother ran a busy home.
Sample Ans.2
My father is a surgeon and my mother is an attorney and former judge.

Q. Do you live with your parents?

Sample Ans.: Yes, I moved back in with my parents after I discovered that more than half my net income was being used to pay for rent and utilities. We have an economic arrangement that allows me to save for my future, while I'm around to help them maintain our home. We all benefit, and we have been able to develop a strong friendship as three adults.

Q. Do you own or rent your home?

Sample Ans.: If you own a house, say so. If you are renting a home, say I am/We are, currently renting a house/unit) in

__________ (name of town), but I'm/we're looking for my/our own home in the area.

Q. How far do you live from this company?

Sample Ans.: I clocked it on my way here today. I'm exactly 10 miles door-to-door, and it took me 17 minutes to get here. A breeze or; with moderate traffic, it took almost an hour. I don't mind commuting that far twice a day. I like to get an early start on my day. If you currently live farther away than what would be considered a reasonable commuting distance, you might mention that you would be willing to locate nearer the company's offices if hired.

Q. Do you speak a foreign language?

(Tips: If you speak another language fluently, by all means, say so. This is an asset. If you took another foreign language in school but cannot remember more than two or three phrases, mention that you have studied that in school or college and enjoyed it, however; you understand the language better than you speak it. You would like to get some language tapes and increase my fluency.)

Q. How much time do you spend with your family?

Sample Ans.: I suppose I spend an average amount. My family is important to me. My great relationship with them gives me the best reason in the world to succeed in my career. In that way, they are an inspiration. I have a responsibility to my job as well as to my family since I've made a strong commitment to both. I like to be there for them when they need me, but they also understand and accept the commitment I have made to my work. So, I spend my time accordingly.

Q. Who is the boss in your family?

Sample Ans. (Tips: Just smile confidently, and say, we operate our family on democratic principles, with the adults making ultimate decisions on what is best for the children. In our family husband and wife are equal partners.)

Q. Is your spouse employed? Will there be a conflict?
Sample Ans. (for married ones): Yes, my (husband/wife) is employed as a ………… We have always been a two-career couple, and we have made the arrangements necessary to accommodate our careers.

Q. What contributed to your divorce? What have you learned from this experience?

Sample Ans.: We married very young and made some mistakes we didn't know how to correct. We lost touch with each other, and eventually, it was too late to salvage anything. I've learned that to earn respect and honesty, you have to communicate openly and be prepared to give honesty and respect. It was a painful lesson, and I have no intention of repeating it.

Q. Do you own a life insurance policy?

Sample Ans.: Yes. I have a family, so a life insurance policy is a must. Or, I am single. No, I don't believe life insurance would be an efficient use of my money now. When I have dependents for whom I am responsible, I will buy life insurance. Right now, I prefer to invest my money.

Q. Do you have a savings plan?

Sample Ans.: Yes, I contribute 5/10 per cent of my net pay to a regular savings account.

Q. Are you in debt?

Sample Ans.: Well, I have a mortgage/ auto loan/charge card balance, but my balance sheet is definitely good. I don't extend my credit beyond what I can afford to pay.

Chapter 12
Open-Ended Questions & Answers

Q. Tell me about yourself.

(Tips: About 80% of all interviews begin with this innocent question. This is one of the most common interview questions asked of both freshers and experienced. The best tip in answering would be to keep it short in the beginning and know how interested is the interviewer to listen and then increase the content. When you hear this question, 'tell me about yourself', answer by pretending that they had asked you, "tell me briefly about your professional experience and the relevant qualities that make you a strong candidate for this job.)

Sample Ans1

After my graduation with honours, I immediately found work with a blue-chip company. I've spent the last five years helping them to grow their B2B market by more than 75%. I'm now ready for a new challenge and a new company.

Sample Ans2.

I grew up in Guntur. When I turned eighteen, I moved to Delhi. There I could also do a Diploma in Computer Applications. While I was working during the day, I completed my MBA at night.

Sample Ans.3

I am among the top graduates of my batch. Besides having a BA/BSc/BCom degree in X subject, I also have an MBA degree in Operations/Digital Business from XYZ Institute. As for my interests, I love exploring new domains, and I'm a fast learner.

Sample Ans.4

I finished my undergrad in 2016 and then started to work for TEMCO Tech as a Software Developer. After 2 years stint there I joined ICCO as Software

Engineer. In 2020, I started my MS in Computer Science at UC. I am presently working on my thesis and I also work as a part-time student researcher at Cardwell R & D Cere.

Sample Ans.5

I am Andrew Bell, a computer graduate from MIT. I like to apply my analytical skills to develop world-class products in the XYZ domain. When I am not working, I volunteer at NGO's as it allows me to serve needy people. I also travel a lot and am an active member of XXX travel group or club through which I could explore my hobby more.

Sample Ans.6
I am one of the top graduates of my batch in college. I am known in school as an organizer, having held several committees and organizations since my first year. I am a dedicated person who never stops working on something until it is perfect. It would be a pleasure for me to discuss how I can be such an asset to your company.

Sample Ans.7
I am a Junior (post), with 2 years of experience. I am responsible for business development activities and last year sold products worth $50,000 to clients. On a day-to-day basis, I also manage a team of up to ten associates. I try to listen to my clients as well as my team.

Sample Ans.8
I'm currently the floor supervisor at Woodhead Shockers. I'm responsible for all aspects of quality control. I run a team of seven staff and am responsible for training, hiring, and firing. The hours can be quite long, but I enjoy it and like the mix of activities from dealing with customers to managing the staff.

Sample Ans.9
For the past few years, I've been deeply dedicated to administrative and managerial work in my organization. In this capacity, I've been lucky to have worn multiple hats like that of a Business Analyst, Team Lead, and Project Manager. I strongly believe in my power of persuasion and people skills. So, I can be a good fit for people-centric roles in your company.

Sample Ans.10

I am John Stuart. Thank you for your time to me. My last school was ZZZ. I did MBA from XXX with a specialization in retail marketing. I worked/working with TTT. During my present/last job, I was instrumental in bringing in three new clients with first-year sales of $6.7 million. We reformed our sales team, and I recruited three new associates. We exceeded our sales goals by 15 per cent! I was responsible for increasing the retail network and sales with my team. I'm excited to be here because of the company's reputation, products/services, work culture and scope to advance my expertise. [Note: If you are currently unemployed, this might also be a good place to share a plausible reason for leaving your last position.]

Sample Ans.11
As a technical project manager, I have more than six years of experience at top Wall Street Companies. In a recent company, I led the development of an award-winning new trading platform. I am a person that survives in a fast-paced environment. At the moment, I am looking for a chance to apply my technical expertise and creative problem-solving skills at an innovative software company like this one.

Sample Ans.12
For the last 4-5 years, I have been deeply involved with my administrative work. I have always been interested in and enjoyed working in the computer industry, but I consider myself lucky that I got an opportunity to work at different levels like business analyst, programmer, and assistant manager. My main strength is the ability to maintain a great rapport with the customer and my attention to their details.

Q. Tell me a little bit more about yourself.
(Tips: In answering, add transitions about your interests to your professional expertise.)

Sample Ans.1
I grew up in Rochester. Then, when I turned eighteen, I moved to Manhattan so that I could major in Photography at the School of Visual Arts. While I was working during the day, I completed

my MBA at night. I really think that the fact that I have both a BA in Photography and an MBA from a great business school makes me the ideal candidate for a management position here at Kodak.

Sample Ans.2
When I'm not working, I like to spend time exploring with my dogs. I take them hiking, visiting historical sites, or even just walking around town. A surprising number of people are drawn to dogs, and I always enjoy talking with those I meet. I feel that communication is one of the most important aspects of my professional life as well. When talking with people, being able to guide the conversation in a particular direction is one of the ways I've been successful in different situations at the office.

Q. What do you consider to be your strongest & weakest points?

Sample Ans.1
I think my greatest strengths are that I am a team player and a master negotiator. I have excellent people skills. Some of my other strong points are that I'm a self-motivated, fast learner. Whatever task I set out to do, I commit myself to it and complete it diligently. However, my biggest weakness is that I trust people quite easily. Also, sometimes I tend to overthink things, but I'm working on bettering myself constantly.

Sample Ans.2
Over the years, I've honed my analytical, critical-thinking, planning, and organizational skills. I can work comfortably in a team or individually. I prioritize work and always ensure that I complete my tasks before the deadline. As for my weak points, I get nervous while speaking in a group, although I'm actively working on it. I hope I can overcome this soon so that I can share my ideas with the entire team and feel like an important part of it.

Q. What is Your Greatest Strength?

Tips: Speak well about yourself as your strength. In answering it, avoid clichés such as: capable, enthusiastic and hard-working. Give concrete examples of things you do well. Talk about attributes that might set you apart from other applicants. Try to sound confident but not over-confident or arrogant.

Sample Ans.1

I am a skilled public relations expert with over XXX years of experience. I have represented and protected my current employer for the last five years. This has included several 'damage limitation' exercises, all of which ended positively for the company. My contribution to the company was rewarded recently with an 'Employee of the Year' award.

Sample Ans. 2

As an office manager with GECO, I have excellent organization skills and really good attention to detail – I'm not the sort of person who does things by half. I also believe that I have good communication skills in dealing with not only external customers but also all members of the internal team – from the senior managers to the junior researchers. As just one example, our company moved offices recently. I had to coordinate the entire move and make sure that our server and all of the computers were set up correctly in the new office. At the same time, I dealt with all of our staff and customers to ensure that day-to-day business was not at all disrupted.

Q. What weaknesses do you have?

(Tips: Weakness should always be something not related to work. Everyone has a weakness. Do not state impractical weaknesses that would make the interviewer feel as if you are an immature person and aren't fit to get this job. Pick up a couple of minor weaknesses that are of little relevance to the job for which you are interviewed. Talk about a weakness that would not affect the job you are applying for. Identify a weakness that you're now in the process of eliminating. Naming a weakness that is strength is the fastest way to come off as inauthentic. When discussing your weaknesses, always talk about how you compensate for them, too. Describe the actions or steps that you take to ensure that your weaknesses don't affect your performance at work.)

Sample Ans.1
My natural tendency is to make up my mind very quickly —and in the past, this has got me into trouble. But I have come to realize that speed is not always appropriate so I always remind myself that I may need to collect more information and weigh up the pros and cons.

Sample Ans.2
Sometimes I lose drive in the middle of a project after the launch excitement has worn off. I combat that by breaking up the project into mini-milestones and celebrating them with my team. The original buzz gets recreated and it becomes obvious how crucial our work is.

Sample Ans.3
Organization management was never my strongest point, but I've recently learned and implemented a time management system that has massively boosted my organizational skills.

Sample Ans.4
I am extremely impatient for quick. I expect my employees to prove themselves on the very first assignment. If they fail, I tend to stop delegating to them and start doing everything by myself. But I realized that it was my weakness. To overcome that weakness, I have started to prep my people on exactly what will be expected of them. I give them the full scope of the assignment and then ask them to discuss where they are on it. At my last job, for example, I was the project manager for a sweepstakes promotion for one of our clients. There were business managers, lawyers, and writers on my team. I broke down all of the tasks into manageable chunks for each employee, then gave them timelines of when they needed to circle back to me. It worked brilliantly and the process helped everyone get the job done, on time and under budget.

Sample Ans.5
My strength is my ability to convert a negative work environment into a positive. At the same time, developing a supportive team. I am also capable of keeping many projects on track and ensuring

deadlines are met. As far as my weakness is concerned, I get impatient sometimes to get everything done very quickly. To tackle the problem, I am trying to re-consider the to-do list and prioritize the tasks.

Sample Ans.6

I am very comfortable working with different groups of people. My strength is my analytical and planning skills, developed over the years. It helps me to complete my work before the deadline. I am a little bit nervous while speaking in a group, but I have given many presentations to overcome this.

Sample Ans.7

I am efficient in many programming languages, including HTML, C++, Java, and AppleScript. I have generated over 100% excess revenue for two separate companies through cost-cutting programming efficiency, and I have leadership experience with a team of five IT professionals working on some of the popular iPhone apps online. As far as weakness is concerned, I tend to remain quiet in meetings, but I am working on speaking up when I feel I have ideas to share.

Sample Ans.8

I'm a highly motivated person. I won't stop until I get things done. I value other people's time and the company's resources. I work to become an asset, not a liability. People say I sometimes act too much as a perfectionist. To counter this, I attended seminars that taught me how to manage myself well.

Q. Do you have any regrets?

Sample Ans.: Sure, I have made mistakes, but I don't think that I have any real regrets. I believe that I've learnt from every situation that I've been in. And those situations and my choices in those situations have made me the person that I am.

Q. What motivates you?

Sample Ans.1 I'm driven by a desire to have a successful career.

Sample Ans2

I'm a very passionate person, and passion is my strongest motivator that continues to push me to become a better version of myself. When it comes to working, I believe that great results will follow if I put in the commitment, dedication, and patience in whatever I do. Working as a part of a team excites me. The thrill of being able to create something valuable motivates me to work harder.

Sample Ans.3

My greatest motivation is to become the best version of what I can be. It excites me to exceed my expectations and accomplish tangible results. I love to be productive and achieve milestones. This gives me a sense of fulfilment and satisfaction. Learning new things and completing new challenges also motivates me to go the extra mile.

Sample Ans.4

I am a very result-oriented person. My primary motivation is to achieve the desired result. While I enjoy working on the project on my own, I am particularly motivated by the buzz of working in a team. It's very exciting working closely with others, who share the same common goal. I also like to take on the challenge and rise to that challenge as part of a concerted team effort.

Sample Ans.5

Primarily, my ability to work hard and deliver results motivates me. But subsequent recognition of my efforts gives me encouragement for my next efforts.

Sample Ans.6

Responsibility towards work motivates me the most, and my aim within any company is to move up to greater levels of responsibility to achieve each goal with better responsibilities.

Sample Ans.7

Many things motivate me. My goal is to be the best of what I can be, which often motivates me to go beyond my expectations.

When I see myself being productive every day, it motivates me to continue.

Q. Has there been a time when you have presented a problem and solved it?

Sample Ans.: Tips: Provide a short and straightforward answer. Start with "Yes. There was a time when...". If you are a fresher having no prior work experience, you can cite examples from school or a personal endeavour that you had in the past.

Chapter 13

Final Questions

Q. Have you ever thought of starting your own business?

Sample Ans.: As I am focused on my career, I do not think about starting my own company. For me, the company I work in is my business. Win or lose, profit or loss, and we are all in the same boat, so my main focus is on the company where my career will grow.

Q. How do you plan to achieve your career goals?

Sample Ans.: For as long as I can remember, I've always been passionate about writing and reading. I've always known that I wanted to be a writer. While my short-term goal is to become a content writer while pursuing my certification in an online digital marketing course, the ultimate goal is to climb the ladder of success and become an editor-in-chief.

Q. You have recently passed out. tell us about your salary expectations.

Sample Ans.: Since I am a fresher, my main goal is to learn and gain experience. As for the salary, I'm sure you will compensate me for matching my knowledge and skills. I am looking forward to growing as a professional with your company, and I'm ready to accept the standard industry salary offered for this position and my skillset.

Q. What salary are you hoping to make in this position?

Sample Ans.: At this early stage, without knowing the details of the position, it's almost impossible for me to cite a figure. Perhaps you could tell me at least the broad parameters of the position and the salary range that has been established at this company for this position. In my experience, similar or identical job titles at various companies don't necessarily mean the same thing, and I'd like to know how the job is described here before attempting to put a dollar figure on it. Furthermore, future opportunities at a company carry as much weight with me as salary and current job description, and both those factors will impact my salary requirement.

Q. What is the salary you think is appropriate for someone with your experience?

Sample Ans.: *If the interviewer continues to pursue the salary topic* -I've determined that my responsibilities are commensurate with the high end of the salary range most employers are willing to pay for this position, which is $_____ to $____.

Q. What is your current salary? what is your salary history?
Tips: You may reply in either of the following ways as it suits you.

Sample Ans.: I shall be happy to tell you, but I'd be more comfortable if you'll allow me first to explain what my current responsibilities are, then ask what the responsibilities of this position are, to better enable both of us to determine if the two positions can be compared monetarily. For me, job fit is as important as money fit, so I'd like to avoid boxing myself in or being excluded at this early stage because of salary restrictions— either mine or yours.

(Note: If you feel you cannot avoid giving an actual figure. Then you may choose from following answers as suits you)

Sample Ans.1
My current employer pays me $_____, which is at the high end of the salary range at the company, and attests to the level of success I have achieved.

Sample Ans.2
Though my current salary is $____, which is lower than many other companies are paying for similar work, it is not a reflection

of my work, but rather a reflection of the fact that my current employer is a small (or start-up) firm just beginning to gain a foothold in this area, and therefore salaries are necessarily lower. I do, however, also receive a yearly bonus and stock options.

Sample Ans.3
My current base salary is $______, but with overtime, end-of-year bonus, company-matched savings plans, pension, and profit sharing, I earn $______, which doesn't account for the complete medical coverage benefit at my current company."

Q. What is your salary expectation? or Do you have any salary expectations? or What salary are you looking for?

(Tips: If you are aware of the salary history of similar jobs in other organizations, don't feel pressured to provide a specific number. Instead, offer a salary range that you would be happy with. At the same time, while stating your salary expectations, ask questions about company benefits, such as healthcare, pensions, vacation etc. If you are aware of the pay structure of the identical position of the company.)

Sample Ans.1
I'm glad you asked me that question. I've taken a look around at similar roles, and I'd be happy to accept a salary in the range of $40,000 to $45,000.

Sample Ans.2
Your priority is the company's growth, not your pay scale. If a company sees me as the potential to increase their stats, then they can opt for increasing my pay.

Sample Ans.3
I'm sure what you're paying is in step with industry norms. Based on what my responsibilities would be, I'm sure we can figure out compensation that makes sense."

Q. What we need to find out is whether we can match the salary you are looking for. What are your salary requirements for accepting this position?

Sample Ans.: I'd prefer to hear your opening offer, based on your knowledge of my capabilities and experience, in conjunction with your knowledge of the salary cap for this position at this company.

Q. What is your current salary, and what percentage increase do you expect to make?

(Tips: Never lie about how much you're currently making. Don't forget, employers have access to the same tools, in addition to personal contacts that enable them to check any information you provide. Be honest about what you're currently making, including non- salary factors, and then base your desired increase on what you know to be the going rate for the job title and whether the new position is a promotion from your current post.)

Sample Ans.: My current yearly salary, including bonuses and benefits, is $__, and I am willing to accept a 15 percent increase over that.

Q. We're prepared to offer you $______? How does that meet with your needs/expectations?
(Tips: If the offer falls short, either of what you're currently making or the percentage increase you were expecting to make, you may say:
Though I'm very excited about the job and the professional opportunities it holds, I am disappointed in your offer. I'm currently making $___, which includes __, ___, __, and ___, and to make the move, I'd need to increase that by at least _____ percent.?)

Q. Instead, we propose a base figure that meets your current salary, and adds stock options. How do you consider it?

Sample Ans.: You'll also need to base your decision on your personal situations. Accepting the job will require relocation to a higher-cost area and therefore need your salary in the form of a biweekly check?

Q. Any question to us? You may ask.

(Tips: Ask inquisitive questions about the job and company. Ask the interviewers to expand on points they may have only touched. Questions relating to the structure of the company, duties of the position, or nature of the product line would all be appropriate here.)

Sample Ans.1
You mentioned earlier that there would be opportunities for relevant professional training. Could you give me more information on this please?

Sample Ans.2
You mentioned you'd be expanding your GECO plant, which would result in about 50 new positions. Is that due to a move away from outside resourcing and to in-house handling? Is this a test, or are there plans for more of this kind of expansion?

Sample Ans.3
You mentioned this position reports to the director of customer service, but you also remarked that it falls within the authority of the marketing department. Is there also a director of marketing to whom I would report?

Sample Ans.4
I had many questions, but you answered them all. You've been so helpful, I'm even more excited about this opportunity than when I applied!

Here is a list of questions you could ask an interviewer:

Q. 400.   Do you expect the primary responsibilities for this position to change in the next six months to a year?
Q. 401.   What are the performance expectations of this position over the first 12 months?